# Bright Line Eating Cookbook

Over 200 proven, delicious & easy to make BLE recipes for losing weight easily and living a happy life!

**Jessica Taylor**

## Copyright 2018 by Jessica Taylor- All rights reserved.

This document is geared towards providing exact and reliable information in regards to the topic and issue covered. The publication is sold on the idea that the publisher is not required to render an accounting, officially permitted, or otherwise, qualified services. If advice is necessary, legal or professional, a practiced individual in the profession should be ordered.

From a Declaration of Principles which was accepted and approved equally by a Committee of the American Bar Association and a Committee of Publishers and Associations.

In no way is it legal to reproduce, duplicate, or transmit any part of this document by either electronic means or in printed format. Recording of this publication is strictly prohibited and any storage of this document is not allowed unless with written permission from the publisher. All rights reserved.

The information provided herein is stated to be truthful and consistent, in that any liability, in terms of inattention or otherwise, by any usage or abuse of any policies, processes, or directions contained within is the solitary and utter responsibility of the recipient reader. Under no circumstances will any legal responsibility or blame be held against the publisher for any reparation, damages, or monetary loss due to the information herein, either directly or indirectly.

Respective authors own all copyrights not held by the publisher.

The information herein is offered for informational purposes solely and is universal as so. The presentation of the information is without a contract or any type of guarantee assurance.

The trademarks that are used are without any consent, and the publication of the trademark is without permission or backing by the trademark owner. All trademarks and brands within this book are for clarifying purposes only and are the owned by the owners themselves, not affiliated with this document.

# Special Bonus

## Are you interested in receiving over 600 delicious recipes for FREE?

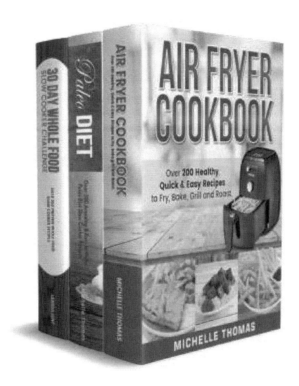

Only sign up for the cookbook box set if you are ready to be absolutely amazed with over 600 proven, delicious and easy to make recipes.

CLICK HERE or copy-paste www.bit.ly/2Ho82AH to get the free box set.

Happy cooking!

# Table of Contents

## Breakfast ..........10
- Breakfast Sandwich ..........11
- Cauliflower Hash Browns ..........11
- Chia Seed Pudding ..........12
- Eggs in Bell Pepper Rings ..........12
- Quinoa Breakfast Scramble ..........13
- Breakfast Parfait ..........13
- Sausage and Peppers Breakfast Casserole ..........14
- Breakfast Cereal ..........15
- Cajun Omelet ..........15
- Chia Pudding with Fruit ..........16
- Gingerbread Oatmeal ..........16
- Mediterranean Omelet ..........17
- Overnight Raspberry Oatmeal ..........18
- Peanut Butter Banana Oatmeal ..........18
- Potato, Spinach, and Red Pepper Frittata ..........19
- Strawberries and Cream Oatmeal ..........19
- Sweet Potato Hash with Sausage & Kale ..........20
- Sweet Potato, Kale & Gruyere Mini Frittatas ..........20
- Vegetable Omelet ..........21
- Yogurt Granola Parfait ..........21
- Yogurt Muesli Bowls ..........22

## Pork & Seafood ..........23
- Grilled Coconut Lime Shrimp and Summer Veggies in Foil ..........24
- Kielbasa, Pepper, Onion and Potato Hash ..........25
- One Pan Baked Cod & Veggies ..........26
- One Pan Italian Sausage and Veggies ..........27
- Saffron Shrimp & Peach Rice Bowls ..........28
- Shrimp Zucchini Noodles ..........29
- Slow Cooker Pork Carnitas ..........30
- Tangerine Grilled Tuna ..........31
- Baked Cod with Olive and Tomato Tapenade ..........32
- Cajun Salmon Zucchini Noodles Salad ..........33
- Ginger Cod ..........33
- Halibut En Papillote ..........34
- Mediterranean Coleslaw and Salmon Bowl ..........35
- Mediterranean Grilled Pork with Tomato-Olive Salsa ..........36
- Miso-Glazed Wild Salmon with Sesame Asparagus ..........37
- Pork & Black Bean Fajitas ..........38
- Pork with Apple and Sweet Potatoes ..........38
- Shrimp and Quinoa Paella ..........39
- Tuna Spiralized Vegetable Salad ..........40

## Poultry ..........41
- Baked Chicken Breasts ..........42
- Bell Pepper Nacho Boats ..........42

| Recipe | Page |
|---|---|
| Caprese Grilled Chicken with Balsamic Reduction | 43 |
| Cheesy Broccoli, Chicken and Rice Bowls | 44 |
| Chicken and Green Chile Egg Muffins | 45 |
| Chicken and Potatoes with Garlic Parmesan Cream Sauce | 46 |
| Chicken and Veggies | 47 |
| Chicken Carnitas Burrito Bowls | 48 |
| Chicken Posole | 50 |
| Creamy Chicken and Mushroom Ragout | 51 |
| Creamy Sun-dried Tomato Chicken | 52 |
| Crock Pot Thai Chicken Curry | 53 |
| Fajita Stuffed Chicken | 54 |
| Grilled Lemon Rosemary Chicken | 55 |
| Jalapeño Turkey Burgers | 55 |
| Italian Skillet Chicken with Tomatoes and Mushrooms | 56 |
| Italian Style Stuffed Zucchini Boats | 57 |
| Lemon Rosemary Chicken | 58 |
| Market Chicken Skillet | 59 |
| One Pot Chicken & Rice Dinner | 60 |
| One Pot Thai Quinoa Bowl with Chicken and Spicy Peanut Sauce | 61 |
| One-Pot Italian Chicken & Quinoa | 62 |
| Ragu Stuffed Portobello Mushrooms | 63 |
| Roasted Chicken and Veggies | 64 |
| Sausage and Veggies | 65 |
| Shredded Chicken Primavera Bowl | 66 |
| Slow Cooker Herb Crusted Turkey Breast | 66 |
| Slow Cooker Enchilada Bake | 67 |
| Slow Cooker Indian Chicken and Rice | 68 |
| Slow Cooker Stuffed Peppers | 69 |
| Taco Potatoes | 70 |
| Thai Chicken Lettuce Cups | 71 |
| Warm Barley, Chickpea, and Tomato Salad with Grilled Chicken | 72 |
| Baked Lemon Chicken | 73 |
| Chicken and Asparagus Stir Fry | 73 |
| Bruschetta Stuffed Chicken Breasts | 74 |
| Buffalo Chicken Wrap | 75 |
| Chicken & Mushroom Risotto | 75 |
| Chicken and Grape Salad | 76 |
| Chicken and Peach Salad | 76 |
| Chicken Bruschetta | 77 |
| Chicken Cacciatore | 77 |
| Chicken Salad Cabbage Wraps | 78 |
| Chipotle Lime Chicken Fajita Skewers | 78 |
| Coconut Garlic Chicken | 79 |
| Garlicky Chicken Thighs in Red Pepper Sauce | 79 |
| Ground Turkey Patties with Tahini Yogurt Sauce | 79 |
| Herbed Chicken & Potatoes | 80 |
| Lemon & Sesame Chicken | 81 |
| Mediterranean Chicken Salad with Fennel, Raisins & Pine Nuts | 82 |
| Mushroom Parmesan Chicken | 83 |

Pan-Seared Tuna Steaks with Warm Tomato, Basil, and Olive Salad ............................................... 84
Pot-Roasted Mediterranean Chicken .................................................................................................. 85
Roasted Red Pepper Chicken ............................................................................................................. 86
Spicy Pecan Crusted Chicken ............................................................................................................. 86
Tahini Chicken Salad ........................................................................................................................... 87
Turkey Chow Mein with Zucchini ....................................................................................................... 87
Turkey Taco Soup ................................................................................................................................ 88
Tuscan Chicken .................................................................................................................................... 88
Vegetable Chicken Soup ..................................................................................................................... 89
Winter Chicken Salad .......................................................................................................................... 89

## Salads .............................................................................................................................................. 90

Asian Quinoa Salad .............................................................................................................................. 91
Avocado Potato Salad ......................................................................................................................... 92
Avocado Salmon Salad with Kale ....................................................................................................... 93
Kale, Carrot and Avocado Salad ........................................................................................................ 93
Bacalao (Salted Cod Salad) ................................................................................................................. 94
Barley and Bean Salad with Herb Pesto ............................................................................................ 95
Chickpea, Avocado, & Feta Salad ....................................................................................................... 96
Cobb Salad ........................................................................................................................................... 96
Grilled Corn & Zucchini Salad with Sun-Dried Tomato Vinaigrette ................................................. 97
Jicama, Black Bean and Quinoa Salad ............................................................................................... 98
Lemon Chicken Breasts with Asparagus & Salad .............................................................................. 99
Mediterranean Salad ......................................................................................................................... 100
Mediterranean Tuna Salad ................................................................................................................ 100
Pan Fried Salmon with Asparagus & Warm Quinoa Salad ............................................................ 101
Quinoa Kale Tomato Corn Salad ...................................................................................................... 102
Shrimp and Feta Salad Bowl ............................................................................................................. 102
Southwest Chickpea Salad ................................................................................................................ 103
Sriracha Lime Chicken Chopped Salad ............................................................................................ 104
Taco Salad in a Jar ............................................................................................................................. 105
Turkey Burgers with Cucumber Salad ............................................................................................. 106
Watermelon, Tomato and Goat Cheese Salad ................................................................................ 107
Zucchini "Pasta" Salad with Pesto, Mozzarella and Tomatoes ..................................................... 108

## Side Dishes ................................................................................................................................... 109

Baked Sweet Potatoes with Crispy Kale and Feta .......................................................................... 110
Cauliflower Fried Rice ....................................................................................................................... 111
Cauliflower Tabbouleh with Green Olives ....................................................................................... 112
Grilled Pumpkin and Carrot over Quinoa ........................................................................................ 113
Italian Oven Roasted Vegetables ..................................................................................................... 114
Mexican-Style Quinoa Salad ............................................................................................................. 115
Risotto with Broccoli Rabe, Ricotta & Toasted Zucchini ................................................................ 116
Spinach & Bean Burrito Wrap .......................................................................................................... 117
Spiralized Raw Zucchini Salad with Avocado and Edamame ........................................................ 118
Sweet Potato Quinoa Cakes ............................................................................................................. 118
Summer Vegetable Tian .................................................................................................................... 119
Zucchini Noodles with Pesto ............................................................................................................ 120
Zucchini Noodles with Pistachio Pesto ............................................................................................ 121
Zucchini Noodles with Spinach and Tomatoes ............................................................................... 122

Greek Roasted Lemon Potatoes ........................................................................................... 123
Leek and Cauliflower Gratin ............................................................................................... 123
Oven Roasted Vegetables ................................................................................................. 124
Quinoa Avocado Salad ..................................................................................................... 124
Quinoa Baked in Red Peppers .......................................................................................... 125
Quinoa Tabbouleh ............................................................................................................. 126
Roasted Green Beans with Lemon, Pine Nuts & Parmigiano ......................................... 126
Soy and Garlic Sautéed Bok Choy .................................................................................... 127
Zucchini Noodles with Creamy Lemon Chive Sauce ....................................................... 127

# Soup .................................................................................................................... 128

Creamy and Spicy Corn Soup ........................................................................................... 129
Hearty Lentil and Vegetable Soup ................................................................................... 130
Sausage and Red Pepper Soup ........................................................................................ 131
Slow Cooker Chickpea Stew with Apricots ..................................................................... 132
Slow Cooker Minestrone ................................................................................................... 133
Slow Cooker Thai Chicken Soup ...................................................................................... 134
Slow Cooker Tomato, Kale and Quinoa Soup ................................................................. 135
White Chicken Chili ........................................................................................................... 136
Arugula Caprese Salad ..................................................................................................... 137
Asian Cucumber & Carrot Salad ...................................................................................... 137
Beet & Spinach Salad ....................................................................................................... 138
Carrot Ginger Soup ........................................................................................................... 138
Classic Creamy Tomato Soup .......................................................................................... 139
Creamy Shrimp Salad ....................................................................................................... 139
Easy Asian Quinoa Salad .................................................................................................. 140
Feta, Peach and Fig Salad ............................................................................................... 140
Garbanzo Bean Salad ....................................................................................................... 141
Garlic Vegetable Soup ...................................................................................................... 141
Greek Chicken Salad ......................................................................................................... 142
Kale, Strawberry and Avocado Salad .............................................................................. 142
Kidney Bean and Cilantro Salad with Vinaigrette .......................................................... 143
Quinoa & Grilled Vegetable Salad with Feta, Olives & Oregano ................................... 144
Savory Carrot, Ginger Squash Soup ................................................................................ 145
Southwestern Cobb Salad ................................................................................................ 146
Spicy Carrot Salad ............................................................................................................. 147
Warm Mushroom and Asparagus Salad .......................................................................... 147
White Chili .......................................................................................................................... 148

# Vegetarian ........................................................................................................... 149

Black Bean and Quinoa Chili Bowl ................................................................................... 150
Burrito in a Jar ................................................................................................................... 151
Quinoa Stir-Fry .................................................................................................................. 151
Instant Pot Enchilada Quinoa .......................................................................................... 152
Mexican Black Bean Casserole ........................................................................................ 153
Quinoa Skillet Supper ....................................................................................................... 154
Roasted Asparagus with Tomato, Halloumi Cheese and Sherry Vinaigrette ................ 155
Roasted Vegetable Quinoa Bowls ................................................................................... 156
Southwestern Broccoli & Potato Casserole .................................................................... 157
Black Bean & Sweet Potato Quinoa ................................................................................. 158

Carrot and Spinach Quinoa Pilaf ................................................................................................................. 159
Chile Con Queso Recipe ............................................................................................................................ 160
Indian Vegetable Curry ............................................................................................................................... 161
Mushroom & Quinoa Sauté ........................................................................................................................ 162
Quinoa with Pomegranates & Butternut Squash ..................................................................................... 162

Bright Line Eating is more than just a diet – it's a revolutionary way to change your life to something that is healthier, happier and free from the imprisoning relationship that you've had with food your whole life.

Bright Line Eating isn't about cabbage soup diets, quick weight loss or special foods. You don't need special apps, or need to count calories or points. Bright Line Eating keeps to four "bright lines". Four principles that will forever change your relationship with food. These bright lines are more than just suggestions, however. These bright lines are clear boundaries that are not to be broken for any reason. Just make the decision right now that there will be no exceptions and do not deviate from that decision. An iron willed commitment to stick with the bright lines – no matter what – is what it will take for you to change your life to become healthier, happier, free and to finally lose – and keep off – the weight you've been battling with.

What are these bright lines? They're very simple – no sugar, no flour, no snacks and no seconds.

First, no sugar. There will still be sugar in your diet in one form and one form only – the kind that comes from consuming a piece of whole fruit with your meal. That's the only kind of sugar you'll be eating from here on out. No sugar, no high fructose corn syrup, honey, agave or even artificial sweeteners. In order for your brain to be rewired to keep the weight off and to clear your brain and get rid of your addiction to food and food cravings, you have to remove all sugar from your diet. That means all sugar in every form, natural and artificial.

Second – no flour. This is for very similar reasons as the no sugar bright line. Flour is highly addictive and changes your brain chemistry. In order to unlock your weight loss and keep your weight off, you need to remove the flour from your diet. This means all forms of flour – flour, starches, and even ground meal (like cornmeal). Whole grains are still a part of your diet, but not the refined or ground grains.

Third – no snacks. You will be eating 3 meals per day (or if necessary, 4 or 5). The bottom line is you'll be eating designated meals every day. Your meals will have a beginning and a definite end. You won't be mindlessly snacking in front of the TV or computer. You consume the food your body needs to function during your meal and that's it.

The final bright line is no seconds. While for some people, you may be able to accomplish this by simply filling your plate once and leaving it at that, for a majority of people that means weighing and measuring everything. This cookbook has included the measurement per serving size. That will help you to know how much of the White Chicken Chili you should be eating in each serving.

When you stick to these four rules, you'll find that your relationship with food, weight loss and health changes drastically. You'll not only begin to lose weight, but you'll keep it off. You may not lose 5 pounds a week, but you also won't be regaining that weight at the end of your crash diet. You'll have a better functioning brain as well. You'll cut out your cravings and allow your body and brain to heal and function at an optimum level.

What are you wait for? Turn the page and get started.

# Breakfast

# Breakfast Sandwich

- 2 sausage patties
- 1 egg, beaten
- 1 Tbs cream cheese
- 2 Tbs sharp cheddar
- 1/4 medium avocado, sliced
- 1/4-1/2 tsp sriracha (to taste)
- Salt, pepper to taste

- Cook the sausage according to package direction.
- Melt together the cream cheese and cheddar cheese.
- Stir in the sriracha and set aside.
- In a small skillet over low heat, cook the egg (seasoned with salt and pepper), without stirring, until nearly set.
- Place the cheese mixture in the omelet and then fold in half and finish cooking until desired doneness.
- Place the egg and avocado in between the sausage patties and serve.

Servings: 1 | Serving Size: 8 oz (entire sandwich)

Calories 472 | Fat 32g | Carbohydrates 13g | Protein 33g

Preparation Time: 10 minutes | Cook Time: 15 minutes

# Cauliflower Hash Browns

- 1 small head grated cauliflower (about 3 cups)
- 1 large Egg
- 3/4 cup Shredded Cheddar Cheese
- 1/4 tsp Cayenne Pepper
- 1/4 tsp garlic powder
- 1/2 tsp salt
- 1/8 tsp black pepper

- Preheat the oven to 400 degrees F and lightly grease a baking sheet.
- Grate the cauliflower and then microwave for 3 minutes.
- Cool slightly and then press out any extra liquid.
- Combine all ingredients and mix well.
- Form into 6 patties and bake on prepared sheet for 15-20 minutes
- Cool for 10 minutes to allow the hash browns to set up before serving.

Servings: 6 | Serving Size: 1 patty

Calories 94 | Fat 6g | Carbohydrates 6g | Protein 6g

Preparation Time: 20 minutes | Cooking Time: 15 minutes | Inactive Time: 10 minutes

# Chia Seed Pudding

- 6 Tbs chia seeds
- 2 cups unsweetened coconut, almond or cashew milk
- blueberries and strawberries, for topping

- Combine the chia seeds and milk and mix well.
- Refrigerate overnight.
- Stir in the berries and serve.

Servings: 2 | Serving Size: 1 cup

Calories 223 | Fat 12g | Carbohydrates 18g | Protein 10g

Preparation Time: 10 minutes

# Eggs in Bell Pepper Rings

- 1 bell pepper, color of choice
- 4 large eggs
- Salt and pepper to taste
- Optional toppings: fresh dill or chives or shredded cheese

- Slice the bell peppers into ½-inch to 1-inch rings.
- Clean out any remaining seeds or membranes.
- Heat a skillet over medium heat and spray with a cooking spray.
- Place the pepper rings in the pan and cook for 1-2 minutes.
- Place an egg into the center of each ring and season with salt and pepper.
- Cook for 3-4 minutes, or until desired doneness.
- Top with toppings of choice and serve.

Servings: 4 | Serving Size: 3.1 oz

Calories 83 | Fat 5g | Carbohydrates 3g | Protein 7g

Preparation Time: 10 minutes | Cooking Time: 10 minutes

# Quinoa Breakfast Scramble

- 1/2 cup cooked quinoa
- 2 eggs scrambled
- 1/2 avocado cubed
- 1 Tbs salsa
- 1/2 tsp lemon pepper
- 1/4 tsp garlic salt

Top the quinoa with the eggs and avocado.

Spread the salsa on top and season to taste with lemon pepper and garlic salt.

Servings: 1 | Serving Size: 11 oz (entire recipe)

Calories 645 | Fat 32g | Carbohydrates 65g | Protein 26g

Preparation Time: 5 minutes | Cooking Time: 5 minutes

# Breakfast Parfait

- 3 cups plain, low fat Greek yogurt
- 3 cups strawberries, hulled and chopped or sliced
- 2 2/3 cup steel cut oats, cooked

- Evenly divide the yogurt among four clear bowls or glasses.
- Top with the strawberries and oats.
- Serve immediately.

Servings: 4 | Yield: 10 oz | Calories 557 | Fat 10g | Carbohydrates 91g | Protein 13g

Preparation Time: 10 minutes

# Sausage and Peppers Breakfast Casserole

- 2 medium red, yellow or orange bell peppers, chopped
- 1 cup chopped red onion, chopped
- 2 cups shredded fontina cheese (8 ounces)
- 1 cup + 2 tablespoons grated Parmesan cheese (divided use)
- 1 lb sweet Italian sausage, crumbled
- 1 Tbs olive oil
- salt
- pepper
- garlic powder
- 8 extra-large eggs
- 1 1/2 cups milk

- Preheat the oven to 375 degrees F. Lightly grease a 9x13 inch pan with cooking spray and set aside.
- Cook the sausage until no pink remains.
- Add the onions and peppers and season with salt, pepper and garlic pepper. Cook for 5-6 minutes, or until tender.
- Combine the sausage mixture with the fontina and 1 cup of parmesan and place in the prepared pan.
- Whisk together the eggs and then whisk in the milk.
- Pour the egg mixture over the sausage mixture and sprinkle on the remaining parmesan.
- Bake for 40 minutes, uncovered, or until a knife inserted in the center comes out clean.
- Let the casserole rest for 5 minutes before serving.

Servings: 12 | Serving Size: 6 oz

Calories 262 | Fat 17g | Carbohydrates 7g | Protein 20g

Preparation Time: 30 minutes | Cooking Time: 50 minutes

# Breakfast Cereal

- 3 cups old fashioned oatmeal, cooked
- 3 cups quinoa, cooked
- 4 cups blackberries

- Combine the oatmeal and quinoa and mix well.
- Evenly divide into four bowls and top with the blackberries before serving.

Servings: 4 | Yield: 10 oz | Calories 228 | Fat 3g | Carbohydrates 43g | Protein 12g

Preparation Time: 5 minutes

# Cajun Omelet

- 4 large eggs
- 1/4 lb spicy sausage
- 1/3 cup mushrooms, sliced
- 1/2 onion, diced
- 1/2 medium bell pepper, chopped
- 2 Tbsp water
- Cooking Fat
- 1 pinch cayenne pepper (optional)
- Sea salt & fresh pepper to taste

- Brown the sausage in a medium saucepan until cooked through.
- Add the mushrooms, onion and bell pepper and cook for another 3-5 minutes, or until tender.
- Meanwhile, whisk together the eggs, water, mustard and spices. Season with the salt and pepper.
- Pour the eggs over the vegetables and reduce heat to low.
- Cook until the top is nearly set and then fold the omelet in half and cover. Cook for another minute before serving hot.

Servings: 2 | Yield: 8.7 oz | Calories 273 | Fat 14g | Carbohydrates 11g | Protein 3g
Preparation Time: 5 minutes | Cooking Time: 8 minutes

# Chia Pudding with Fruit

- ¼ cup chia seeds
- 1 cup light coconut milk
- ½ cup diced mango

- Mix together the chia seeds and milk.
- Refrigerate overnight.
- Add the fruit and serve.

Servings: 1 | Yield: 12.9 oz (entire recipe) | Calories 495 | Fat 33g | Carbohydrates 44g | Protein 21g
Preparation Time: 5 minutes | Inactive Time: 12 hours

# Gingerbread Oatmeal

- 1/3 cup quick oats
- 1/2 banana
- 1/4 tsp ginger ground
- 1/8 tsp cinnamon ground
- small sprinkle nutmeg ground
- small sprinkly cloves ground
- 1 Tbs almond butter

- Combine the oats and water.
- Microwave for 45 seconds, then stir and cook for another 30-45 seconds.
- Stir in the spices and drizzle on the almond butter before serving.

Servings: 1 | Yield: 3.8 oz (entire recipe) | Calories 246 | Fat 11g | Carbohydrates 33g | Protein 6g
Preparation Time: 5 minutes | Cooking Time: 2 minutes

# Mediterranean Omelet

- 1 Tbs olive oil
- ¼ cup bell pepper, diced
- 2 cup spinach, chopped
- ¼ cup tomato, diced
- ¼ cup kalamata olives, sliced
- **Eggs**
- 2 tsp cooking oil, divided
- 6 eggs, whisked and divided
- **Toppings**
- ¼ cup crumbled feta (optional)
- ¼ cup tomato, diced
- ¼ cup kalamata olives, sliced
- Parsley leaves
- Salt and pepper, to taste

- Sauté the bell pepper in 1 tsp olive oil for 3 minutes over medium high heat in a medium sized skillet.
- Add the spinach, tomatoes and olives and cook for 1-2 minutes. Set aside.
- In a separate skillet, heat the remaining oil on medium low.
- Add half of the egg mixture to the pan and swirl the pan to coat it with the eggs.
- Cook for 2-3 minutes, or until nearly set and then top with half of the vegetables on one half of the egg mixture.
- Fold the omelet in half and cook for 1-2 minutes, or until done.
- Repeat with the remaining omelet and serve hot.

Servings: 2 | Yield: 10 oz | Calories 427 | Fat 34g | Carbohydrates 6g | Protein 1g
Preparation Time: 5 minutes | Cooking Time: 10 minutes

# Oatmeal Cookie Breakfast Smoothie

- 1 yellow banana sliced and frozen
- 3/4 cup milk
- 1/4 cup ice
- 2 Tbs rolled oats
- 2 tsp almond butter
- 1/8 tsp vanilla
- 1/2 tsp cinnamon
- Small sprinkle ground nutmeg optional

- Combine all Ingredients in a blender and blend until smooth.

Servings: 1 | Yield: 12.1 oz (entire recipe) | Calories 336 | Fat 11g | Carbohydrates 54g | Protein 10g

Preparation Time: 5 minutes

# Overnight Raspberry Oatmeal

- 1/2 cup old fashioned oats
- 2/3 cup skim milk
- 1/2 cup plain Greek yogurt
- 1 Tbs chia seeds
- 1/2 tsp vanilla
- 1/2 cup fresh raspberries
- 1 medium banana
- 1 tsp coconut, for garnish

- Combine the oats, milk, yogurt, chia seeds and vanilla in a bowl with a lid.
- Refrigerate for 12 hours.
- Top with fruit and coconut before serving.

Servings: 2 | Yield: 10.6 oz | Calories 282 | Fat 6g | Carbohydrates 48g | Protein 10g
Preparation Time: 2 minutes | Inactive Time: 12 hours

# Peanut Butter Banana Oatmeal

- 1/3 cup quick oats
- 1/4 tsp cinnamon (optional)
- 1/2 banana, sliced
- 1 Tbs peanut butter, unsweetened

- Combine all ingredients in a bowl with a lid.
- Refrigerate for 12 hours, then serve warm or cold.

Servings: 1 | Yield: 3.8 oz (entire recipe) | Calories 245 | Fat 10g | Carbohydrates 34g | Protein 5g
Preparation Time: 5 minutes | Cooking Time: 2 minutes

# Potato, Spinach, and Red Pepper Frittata

- 1 lb potatoes
- ¼ cup olive oil
- 1 clove garlic, minced
- 1 small red bell pepper, seeded, and thinly sliced
- 1 small yellow onion, thinly sliced
- 2 cups baby spinach
- 3 Tbs unsalted butter, cubed
- Kosher salt and freshly ground black pepper, to taste
- 2 Tbs thinly sliced basil
- 8 eggs, beaten

- Steam the potatoes until tender.
- In an oven proof skillet, sauté the garlic, pepper and onion for 3-4 minutes in the butter.
- Add the spinach and cook for an additional minute.
- Add the potatoes, butter, salt, pepper, half of the basil and eggs.
- Cook for 8-10 minutes on low, or until nearly set.
- Broil for 3 minutes, or until set and golden brown.
- Garnish with basil before serving.

Servings: 8 | Yield: 5.5 oz | Calories 233 | Fat 15g | Carbohydrates 8g | Protein 0g
Preparation Time: 10 minutes | Cooking Time: 20 minutes

# Strawberries and Cream Oatmeal

- 1/3 cup quick oats
- 1/2 cup strawberries
- 1/2 cup plain yogurt

- Combine all ingredients in a bowl with a lid.
- Refrigerate for 12 hours, then serve warm or cold.

Servings: 1 | Yield: 8.1 oz | Calories 188 | Fat 4g | Carbohydrates 30g | Protein 4g
Preparation Time: 5 minutes | Cooking Time: 2 minutes

# Sweet Potato Hash with Sausage & Kale

- 4 small sweet potatoes, chopped
- 2 apples, cored and chopped
- 1 lb sausage, ground
- 1 clove garlic, minced
- 10 oz kale, chopped
- Salt & pepper

- Brown the sausage until no pink remains.
- Add the remaining ingredients. Cook for an additional 5-6 minutes, or until the kale and apples are tender.
- Season to taste and serve hot.

Servings: 4 | Yield: 15 oz | Calories 544 | Fat 23g | Carbohydrates 65g | Protein 11g
Preparation Time: 5 minutes | Cooking Time: 15 minutes

# Sweet Potato, Kale & Gruyere Mini Frittatas

- 1 Tbs olive oil
- 2 cups kale, chopped small
- 1 clove garlic, minced or grated with a microplane
- pinch of kosher salt and fresh ground pepper
- 1 small sweet potato, diced small (about 1 cup)
- 1 tsp cumin
- 1 tsp dried oregano
- pinch of salt and freshly ground pepper
- 6 eggs, lightly beaten
- 2 Tbs whole milk
- 1 cup grated gruyere (on the mid sized holes of a box grater), about 3 oz, divided

- Preheat the oven to 350 degrees F and lightly grease 24 mini muffin cups.
- Sauté the kale and garlic in the oil over medium high heat. Season with salt and pepper and cook for 2 minutes
- Remove from the pan and set aside.
- Add the sweet potato, oregano and cumin to the skillet and cook for 5-6 minutes.
- Add the eggs, milk and half of the cheese to the kale and mix well. Season with salt and pepper.
- Evenly divide the mixture into the cups.
- Top with the sweet potato, cheese, salt and pepper.
- Bake for 15 minutes, then cool for 5 minutes before removing and serving.

Servings: 8 | Yield: 3.2 oz | Calories 151 | Fat 10g | Carbohydrates 6g | Protein 1g
Preparation Time: 10 minutes | Cooking Time: 20 minutes

# Vegetable Omelet

- 6 eggs
- 1 cup mixed vegetables
- cooking spray
- salt & pepper to taste

- Pour the eggs into a greased skillet and cook on low until the eggs are nearly set.
- Add the vegetables to one half of the omelet and then fold the omelet in half.
- Continue to cook until set up. Cut in half and serve.

Servings: 2 | Yield: 13.3 oz | Calories 381 | Fat 16g | Carbohydrates 32g | Protein 9g
Preparation Time: 5 minutes | Cooking Time: 20 minutes

# Yogurt Granola Parfait

- 6 oz non-fat Greek vanilla flavored yogurt
- 1/4 cup steel cut oats, cooked
- 1/4 cup dried fruit mix
- 1/4 cup blueberries and raspberries

- Top the yogurt with the cereal and fruit. Serve immediately.

Servings: 1 | Yield: 10.5 oz (entire recipe) | Calories 294 | Fat 4g | Carbohydrates 54g | Protein 3g

Preparation Time: 2 minutes

# Yogurt Muesli Bowls

- **Muesli**
  - 1 cup rolled oats
  - 1 Tbs Chia Seed (optional)
  - 1/4 cup almonds
  - 1/4 cup nuts

- **Tropical Yogurt**
  - 1 banana
  - 1 lime, juiced
  - 8 oz plain yogurt
  - 1 tsp coconut oil
  - pinch cinnamon
  - 1-2 mint leaves (optional)
  - Mint to garnish (3-4 mint leaves)
  - Lime Zest
  - Optional unsweetened coconut flakes on top!

- Combine the muesli ingredients and set aside.
- Combine the yogurt ingredients and mix well.
- Top the yogurt with the muesli.
- Refrigerate for at least 2 hours before serving.

Servings: 3 | Yield: 6.6 oz | Calories 338 | Fat 16g | Carbohydrates 39g | Protein 8g
Preparation Time: 5 minutes | Inactive Time: 2 hours

# Pork & Seafood

# Grilled Coconut Lime Shrimp and Summer Veggies in Foil

- 1 small yellow onion, chopped
- 2 garlic cloves
- 1 cup shredded unsweetened coconut
- zest and juice of 1 lime
- 1 cup fresh cilantro or parsley, chopped
- 1/4- cup olive oil
- 1/4- cup soy sauce
- 1 lb raw shrimp, peeled and deveined
- 1 zucchini, sliced into 1/4-inch rounds
- 1 to 2 cups corn
- chopped fresh cilantro or parsley, for garnish

- Combine the onions, garlic, coconut, lime zest, lime juice, cilantro, olive oil and soy sauce in a blender. Puree.
- Add to a resealable bag with the shrimp and refrigerate for 2-4 hours.
- Make 2 packets of foil and place half of the shrimp and vegetables in each one.
- Fold up the sides to seal and grill for 10-12 minutes.
- Serve, garnished with cilantro or parsley.

Servings: 6 | Serving Size: 7 oz

Calories 255 | Fat 18g | Carbohydrates 12g | Protein 13g

Preparation Time: 2 hours | Cooking Time: 15 minutes

# Kielbasa, Pepper, Onion and Potato Hash

- 1 (14 ounce) package turkey sausage, cut into 1/4 inch rounds
- 1 green bell pepper, diced
- 1/2 yellow, red or orange bell pepper, diced
- 1 onion, diced
- 3 small or 2 large potatoes, peeled and diced
- olive oil
- salt and pepper

- Heat 2 Tbs of olive oil in a heavy skillet over medium high heat.
- Season the potatoes with salt and pepper and cook for 8-10 minutes, or until golden brown.
- Meanwhile, brown the sausage for 5 minutes in another tablespoon of oil. Set aside.
- Sauté the onions and peppers in the sausage skillet for 5 minutes, or until softened.
- Season to taste with salt and pepper.
- Combine the potatoes, sausage, onions and peppers and serve hot.

Servings: 4 | Serving Size: 11 oz

Calories 363 | Fat 20g | Carbohydrates 31g | Protein 16g

Preparation Time: 5 minutes | Cooking Time: 10 minutes

*Note: Applegate organic turkey sausage is sugar free.

# One Pan Baked Cod & Veggies

- 1 lb atlantic cod divided into 4 pieces
- 2 cups Cherry Tomatoes
- 2 cups purple potatoes diced
- 3-4 Tbs oil
- seasoning as desired (Italian seasoning suggested)

- Preheat the oven to 400 degrees F.
- Combine the potatoes and half of the oil.
- Roast for 15 minutes, then add the tomatoes and cod to the pan.
- Drizzle on the remaining oil, then season with salt, pepper and additional spices of choice.
- Bake for another 10-12 minutes and serve hot.

Servings: 4 | Serving Size: 8.7 oz

Calories 228 | Fat 11g | Carbohydrates 10g | Protein 22g

Preparation Time: 5 minutes | Cooking Time: 25 minutes

# One Pan Italian Sausage and Veggies

- 2 cups large carrots, thinly sliced
- 2 cups red potatoes, diced
- 2 1/3 cups zucchini, thickly sliced
- 2 cups red peppers, chopped
- 1 ½ cups broccoli florrets
- 1 lb Italian sausage, thickly sliced
- Seasonings
- 1/2 Tbs EACH: dried basil, dried oregano, dried parsley, garlic powder
- 1/2 tsp EACH: onion powder, dried thyme
- 1/8 tsp red pepper flakes optional
- 1/3 cup Parmesan cheese freshly grated, optional
- 4 and 1/2 tablespoons olive oil
- Optional: fresh parsley, salt and pepper

- Preheat the oven to 400 degrees F. Line a sheet pan with foil or parchment paper and set aside.
- Combine all the seasonings and olive oil in a bowl.
- Add the sausage and veggies to the seasonings and mix well.
- Spread onto the sheet pan and bake for 15 minutes.
- Stir and bake for another 10-20 minutes, or until the vegetables are tender.
- Serve, garnished with parmesan cheese and parsley, if desired.

Servings: 6 | Serving Size: 9.6 oz

Calories 304 | Fat 19g | Carbohydrates 19g | Protein 16g

Preparation Time: 15 minutes | Cooking Time: 30 minutes

*Note: Applegate organic Italian sausage does not contain sugar.

# Saffron Shrimp & Peach Rice Bowls

- 1 1/2 cups uncooked brown rice (long or short grained)
- 3 cups low-sodium chicken or vegetable broth
- 1 lb large raw shrimp, shelled
- 2 firm, ripe peaches, pitted and chopped
- 1 clove garlic, peeled and sliced
- 1/8 tsp saffron threads
- 1/4 tsp paprika
- 1/8 tsp cayenne pepper
- 1/4 tsp kosher or sea salt
- 1 Tbs fresh squeezed lime juice
- 1/2 cup coarsely chopped cilantro leaves
- 2 Tbs extra-virgin olive oil
- 1 lime, cut into 4 wedges for serving

- Bring the broth and rice to a boil. Reduce heat to low and cook, covered, for 35 minutes, or until the liquid is absorbed and the rice is tender.
- Mix together the peaches and 1 Tbs of lime juice and then set aside.
- Sauté the shrimp in the oil and season with salt, paprika, cayenne pepper and saffron. Cook for 3 minutes.
- Add the garlic and cook for another minute, or until the shrimp is pink and opaque. Remove from the heat.
- Place the rice into 4 bowl and top with the shrimp and peaches.
- Garnish with cilantro and lemon wedges before serving.

Servings: 8 | Serving Size: 8.5 oz

Calories 232 | Fat 6g | Carbohydrates 36g | Protein 12g

Preparation Time: 10 minutes | Cooking Time: 35 minutes

# Shrimp Zucchini Noodles

- 2 Tbs unsalted butter
- 2 Tbs olive oil
- 1 lb medium shrimp, peeled and deveined
- 1 shallot, minced
- 4 cloves garlic, minced
- 1/4 tsp red pepper flakes, or more, to taste
- Kosher salt and freshly ground black pepper, to taste
- 1/4 cup vegetable stock
- 2 Tbs freshly squeezed lemon juice
- 1 tsp lemon zest
- 1 1/2 lbs (4 medium-sized) zucchini, spiralized
- 2 Tbs freshly grated Parmesan

- Heat the butter and olive oil in a skillet over medium high heat.
- Cook the shrimp, shallot, garlic, red pepper flakes, salt and pepper for 2-3 minutes, or until the shrimp is pink.
- Stir in the stock, lemon juice and lemon zest.
- Season with salt and pepper and then bring to a simmer.
- Stir in the zucchini noodles and cook for 1-2 minutes, or until tender.
- Serve immediately, garnished with Parmesan, if desired.

Servings: 4 | Serving Size: 15 oz

Calories 311 | Fat 15g | Carbohydrates 25g | Protein 21g

Preparation Time: 25 minutes | Cooking Time: 10 minutes

# Slow Cooker Pork Carnitas

- 1 Tbs chili powder
- 2 tsp ground cumin
- 2 tsp dried oregano
- 2 tsp salt, or more, to taste
- 1 tsp ground black pepper
- 4 lb pork shoulder, excess fat trimmed
- 4 cloves garlic, peeled
- 2 onions, quartered
- 2 oranges, juiced
- 2 limes, juiced

- Combine the chili powder, cumin, oregano, salt and pepper in a small bowl and mix well.
- Rub the pork shoulder with the spice mixture on all sides.
- Combine the pork shoulder, garlic, onions, orange and lime juices into a slow cooker.
- Cook on low for 8 hours or high for 4-5 hours.
- Shred the pork and then return to the pot.
- Season with salt and pepper and cook for another 30 minutes.
- Broil the pork for 3-4 minutes, if desired, to crisp the pork before serving with sides of choice.

Servings: 8 | Serving Size: 11.5 oz

Calories 469 | Fat 28g | Carbohydrates 12g | Protein 41g

Preparation Time: 10 minutes | Cooking Time: 8 hours and 30 minutes

# Tangerine Grilled Tuna

- 2 Tuna steaks (4 oz each)
- 1/2 cup Watercress
- 10 Cherry tomatoes, halved
- 1 tsp olive oil (for drizzle)
- For marinade:
- 2 oz tangerine juice
- 1 tsp sea salt
- 1 tsp ground black peppercorn
- 1 tsp ground ginger

- For Tangerine Carrot Dressing
- 2 Tbs olive oil
- 1 tsp ground ginger
- 1 tsp roasted garlic
- 4 oz chopped red onions
- 1 cup baby carrots
- Juice of 1 tangerine
- Salt and pepper to taste

- Combine the marinade ingredients and pour over the tuna in a resealable bag or a deep dish.
- Refrigerate for 1 hour.
- Meanwhile, combine the dressing ingredients in a blender and puree.
- Combine 2 Tbs dressing with the watercress and tomatoes and mix well. Refrigerate until serving.
- Grease the grill with the olive oil and grill the tuna for 4-6 minutes per side on medium high heat.
- Place the tuna on the salad to serve.

Servings: 2 | Serving Size: 1 tuna steak & half of salad

Calories 421 | Fat 0g | Carbohydrates 40g | Protein 24g

Preparation Time: 10 minutes | Cooking Time: 15 minutes | Inactive Time: 1 hour

*Note: Tuna is a little drier fish, so be careful not to overcook the meat. 4 minutes per side will be more rare, but do not overcook the meat.

# Baked Cod with Olive and Tomato Tapenade

- 1 lb cod, cut into 4 fillets
- 1 cup cherry tomatoes, halved
- 1/3 cup prepared olive tapenade
- 1 large shallot, minced
- 1 garlic clove, minced
- 1 Tbs balsamic vinegar
- 1 Tbs olive oil
- 2 tsp dried organo
- 1 tsp paprika
- 2 Tbs fresh chives, chopped
- Salt & pepper to taste

- Preheat the oven to 425 degrees F. Line a baking sheet with parchment paper.
- Season the cod with the ½ Tbs olive oil, paprika, salt and pepper.
- Bake for 20 minutes, or until tender.
- While the fish is cooking, sauté the shallot and garlic in the olive oil over medium high heat for 30 seconds.
- Add the tomatoes and oregano and continue to cook for another 3-4 minutes, or until the tomatoes soften slightly.
- Add the balsamic vinegar and stir, then remove from the heat.
- Top the fish with the tapenade and then the seasoned tomatoes before serving, garnished with chives.

Servings: 4 | Yield: 9.6 oz | Calories 225 | Fat 6g | Carbohydrates 20g | Protein 4g
Preparation Time: 10 minutes | Cooking Time: 20 minutes

# Cajun Salmon Zucchini Noodles Salad

- 2 zucchini, spiral sliced
- 1 cup red onion, chopped
- 1 cup diced/sliced cherry tomatoes
- 1 Tbs lemon juice
- Salt/pepper to taste
- 1/2 cup mayonnaise
- 1/2 Tbs olive oil
- 1/2 tsp paprika
- 1 tsp minced garlic
- 1/4 tsp salt/pepper
- 1/8 tsp onion powder
- 1/4 tsp cayenne
- 5 oz salmon, cooked
- Fresh Cilantro (torn) to garnish
- 2 Tbs capers
- 1 Tbs crushed red pepper flakes to garnish

- Combine the vegetables and zucchini noodles and season with the lemon juice and pepper.
- Whisk together the mayonnaise, oil, paprika, garlic, onion powder, cayenne, salt and pepper. Season with additional spices to taste.
- Drizzle the dressing over the vegetables.
- Serve topped with the salmon and garnished with the red pepper, capers and cilantro.

Servings: 3 | Yield: 12.1 oz | Calories 231 | Fat 14g | Carbohydrates 19g | Protein 3g

Preparation Time: 10 minutes

# Ginger Cod

- 3 Tbs low-sodium soy sauce
- 2 Tbs fresh lemon juice
- 1 tsp sesame oil
- 1 tsp grated fresh ginger
- 1 clove garlic, grated
- 4 (5- to 6-ounce) sablefish (black cod) filets

- Combine all ingredients, except cod, and mix well.
- Pour the marinade over the cod in a shallow dish and marinate for 30 minutes, refrigerated.
- Pan fry over medium heat for 5 minutes per side, or until the fish is cooked through.
- Meanwhile, bring the marinade to a boil in a small saucepan and cook until it is reduced.
- Serve the fish with the sauce over it.

Servings: 4 | Yield: 5.8 oz | Calories 124 | Fat 2g | Carbohydrates 1g | Protein 0g
Preparation Time: 5 minutes | Cooking Time: 10 minutes | Inactive Time: 30 minutes

# Halibut En Papillote

- 4 Tbs unsalted butter, softened
- 4 cloves garlic, minced
- 2 tsp fresh oregano, minced
- 1/4 tsp red pepper flakes
- 1/2 tsp salt
- 1/4 tsp pepper
- 4 zucchinis, sliced
- 4 medium carrots, sliced
- 2 medium red peppers, sliced
- 8 sheets parchment paper (16 x 14 inches each)
- 8 pieces halibut fillet (8 oz each)
- 1/2 cup fresh basil, chopped
- Lemon wedges for serving, if desired

- Preheat the oven to 450 degrees F.
- Combine the butter, garlic, oregano, red pepper flakes, salt and pepper in a bowl and mix well.
- Evenly divide the vegetables among the parchment papers, then top with the fish.
- Drizzle on the butter mixture and fold the parchment paper into little envelopes, taking care to crimp the edges.
- Bake, on a baking sheet, for 15 minutes.
- Season with basil and lemon before serving.

Servings: 8 | Yield: 12.9 oz | Calories 406 | Fat 13g | Carbohydrates 13g | Protein 5g
Preparation Time: 15 minutes | Cooking Time: 15 minutes

# Mediterranean Coleslaw and Salmon Bowl

**For the coleslaw dressing**
- 1 large lemon, juiced
- 2 Tbsp white wine vinegar
- 1/2 cup olive oil
- 4 cloves garlic, chopped
- salt and pepper to taste
- 1 Tbsp ground sumac, or to taste
- 1 Tbsp dried oregano
- 1 tsp crushed red pepper flakes

**For the Coleslaw**
- 1/2 head green cabbage head, thinly sliced or chopped
- 1/2 head whole red cabbage head, thinly sliced or chopped
- 2 carrots, grated
- 6 radishes, trimmed, chopped or sliced into thin sticks
- 2 celery sticks, chopped
- 3 green onions, trimmed, and chopped (both the green and white parts)
- 2 cups chopped parsley leaves
- 2 cups chopped mint leaves
- 2 Tbsp freshly grated ginger root
- 14 oz chickpeas (optional, to be added at the end)

**For the Salmon**
- 1 1/2 lbs Salmon Fillet (or 4 6-oz salmon fillet pieces)
- Salt and pepper
- 1 tsp garlic powder

- Preheat the oven to 425 degrees F and lightly grease a baking sheet. Season the salmon and bake for 15-20 minutes, or until tender.
- Combine the dressing ingredients and mix well. Set aside.
- Add the dressing to the coleslaw ingredients and mix well. Evenly divide the coleslaw into six portions and top with the salmon. Serve

Servings: 6 | Yield: 14.1 oz | Calories 436 | Fat 27g | Carbohydrates 24g | Protein 8g
Preparation Time: 20 minutes | Cooking Time: 20 minutes

# Mediterranean Grilled Pork with Tomato-Olive Salsa

- **For the spice rub:**
- 2 tsp crushed or chopped fennel seeds
- 1-1/2 tsp sweet paprika
- 1-1/2 tsp garlic powder
- 1-1/2 tsp freshly ground black pepper
- 1 tsp kosher salt
- **For the salsa:**
- 2 scant cups cherry (or grape) tomatoes, quartered
- 1/2 small red onion, cut into small dice (about 1/2 cup)
- 1/4 cup coarsely chopped pimento-stuffed green olives
- 2 Tbs drained capers
- 2 Tbs torn fresh basil leaves
- 1 large clove garlic, minced
- 1 Tbs extra-virgin olive oil
- 2 tsp fresh lemon juice; more to taste
- 1/2 tsp finely grated lemon zest
- Kosher salt and freshly ground black pepper
- 6 boneless pork loin chops, about 3/4 inch thick
- 1-1/2 Tbs canola or vegetable oil

- Combine the rub and season the pork with the rub.
- Combine the tapenade ingredients and mix well.
- Grill the pork over medium high heat for 3-4 minutes per side, or until cooked through.
- Serve the pork topped with the tapenade.

Servings: 8 | Yield: 4.8 oz | Calories 151 | Fat 7g | Carbohydrates 4g | Protein 2g
Preparation Time: 10 minutes | Cooking Time: 10 minutes

# Miso-Glazed Wild Salmon with Sesame Asparagus

- 1/2 cup white miso
- 1/4 cup dry sake or dry white wine
- 2 tbsp mirin
- 1 Tbs soy sauce
- 2 tsp finely grated fresh ginger
- 1 1-1/2- to 2-lb. skin-on wild salmon fillet, pin bones removed
- 1-1/2 lb medium-thick asparagus, trimmed
- 2 tsp vegetable oil; more as needed
- Kosher salt
- 1 tsp Asian sesame oil
- 1-1/2 tsp toasted sesame seeds
- 1 handful cherry tomatoes (optional)

- Combine the marinade ingredients and spread over the salmon. Marinate for at least 30 minutes.
- Season the asparagus with oil, salt and pepper.
- Place the asparagus and salmon on a baking sheet lined with parchment paper.
- Broil for 2-4 minutes, then toss the asparagus and cook for another 2-3 minutes. Continue to toss and cook the asparagus until the salmon and asparagus are tender.
- Drizzle with the sesame oil and garnish with sesame seeds before serving.

Servings: 5 | Yield: 15.2 oz | Calories 326 | Fat 14g | Carbohydrates 52g | Protein 3g
Preparation Time: 10 minutes | Cooking Time: 10 minutes

# Pork & Black Bean Fajitas

- 3 green peppers, sliced
- 1 can black beans, rinsed and drained
- 1 onion, sliced
- 1 Tbs Apple Cider Vinegar
- 1 Tbs Chili Powder
- 2 tsp ground cumin
- 1 tsp paprika
- 1/4 tsp crushed red pepper flakes
- 1 lb pork loin, fat trimmed and sliced into 1" slices

- Combine all ingredients in a slow cooker and cook on low for 8 hours.
- Serve hot, topped with lettuce and shredded cheese.

Servings: 4 | Yield: 12.9 oz | Calories 328 | Fat 5g | Carbohydrates 35g | Protein 13g
Preparation Time: 2 minutes | Cooking Time: 8 hours

# Pork with Apple and Sweet Potatoes

- 1 lb pork loin, sliced or cubed
- 2 Sweet potatoes – peeled and cut into bit size pieces
- 2 tart apples, diced
- 1/2 cup onion – chopped
- 2 cloves garlic – minced
- 2 tsp apple cider vinegar
- 1 Tbs Curry Powder
- 1/2 tsp ground ginger
- salt & pepper to taste

- Combine all ingredients in a slow cooker and cook on low for 8 hours.
- Serve hot.

Servings: 4 | Yield: 10.4 oz | Calories 296 | Fat 4g | Carbohydrates 37g | Protein 6g
Preparation Time: 2 minutes | Cooking Time: 6 hours

# Shrimp and Quinoa Paella

- 1 lb uncooked shrimp
- 1 cup quinoa, rinsed
- 1 large yellow onion, finely chopped
- 2 medium-large sized zucchini, chopped
- 2 1/2 cups fat free chicken broth
- 1 cup peas, fresh or frozen
- 1 large bell pepper, cut into strips
- 1/2 cup sun-dried tomatoes (not packed in oil)
- 3 garlic cloves, mined
- 1 Tbs olive oil
- 1 tsp smoked paprika
- Generous pinch of saffron threads
- 1 bay leaf
- 1 tsp crushed red pepper flakes
- Zest from 1 lemon
- Salt & pepper to taste

- Sauté the onions and garlic for 2 minutes in the oil in a large skillet over medium high heat.
- Add the peppers and cook for an additional 3 minutes.
- Add quinoa, broth, saffron, bay leaf, paprika, red pepper flakes, lemon zest, salt and pepper. Bring ot a boil, then reduce heat to simmer for 12-15 minutes, or until the liquid is absorbed.
- Add the remaining ingredients and cook for 5-8 minutes, or until the shrimp is no longer pink. Season to taste with additional salt and pepper before serving.

Servings: 6 | Yield: 12.7 oz | Calories 275 | Fat 5g | Carbohydrates 35g | Protein 5g
Preparation Time: 15 minutes | Cooking Time: 30 minutes

# Tuna Spiralized Vegetable Salad

- 3 baby turnips, spiralized
- 2 cucumber, spiralized
- 1 tsp minced Garlic (about 3 cloves)
- 1/4 cup chopped shallot or red onion
- 1/4 cup paleo mayo (see notes for other options)
- 1 tsp mustard powder
- 1 small chili red pepper or cayenne pepper - sliced
- 2-3 tbsp olive oil with a pinch of ground chili pepper mixed in it
- salt/pepper to taste
- cilantro to garnish
- red pepper flakes or a pinch of cayenne to top
- 5 oz wild caught canned tuna (drained)

- Combine the mayonnaise, mustard, lemon juice, garlic, onion, salt and pepper.
- Combine the vegetables and mayonnaise mixture and mix well.
- Season the tuna with oil and chili pepper.
- Add the tuna and mix well. Season to taste and serve, garnished with cilantro.

Servings: 3 | Yield: 16.9 oz | Calories 272 | Fat 15g | Carbohydrates 21g | Protein 5g

Preparation Time: 10 minutes

# Poultry

# Baked Chicken Breasts

- 4 boneless, skinless chicken breasts
- 2 Tbs Extra Virgin Olive Oil
- 1 tsp kosher salt
- 1/2 tsp black pepper
- 1/2 tsp garlic powder
- 1/2 tsp onion powder
- 1/2 tsp chili powder

- Preheat the oven to 450 degrees F. Lightly grease a 9x13-inch baking dish.
- Pound the chicken breasts until they are an even ¾-inch thick.
- Lightly coat the chicken with olive oil.
- Whisk together the salt, pepper, garlic powder, onion powder and chili powder.
- Season the chicken on both sides with the spice mixture and place in the prepared pan.
- Bake for 15-20 minutes, or until the chicken is cooked through.
- Rest for 5-10 minutes, covered with foil, then slice and serve.

Servings: 4 | Serving Size: 1 chicken breast (3 oz)

Calories 205 | Fat 10g | Carbohydrates 1g | Protein 27g

Preparation Time: 5 minutes | Cooking Time: 15 minutes

# Bell Pepper Nacho Boats

- 1 lb lean ground turkey
- 1 tsp chili powder
- 1 tsp cumin
- 1/2 tsp black pepper
- 1/4 tsp kosher or sea salt
- 3/4 cup salsa
- 1 cup grated cheddar cheese, reduced-fat
- 9 mini bell peppers

- Preheat the oven to 375 degrees F. Line a pan with parchment paper and set aside.
- Slice the mini bell peppers in half and remove any seeds and membranes.
- Cook the turkey in a skillet over medium high heat until cooked through. Drain.
- Combine the turkey, spices and salt and mix well.
- Place the turkey mixture in the bell pepper boats and sprinkle on the cheese.
- Bake on the prepared pan for 10 minutes, or until the cheese is melted and the peppers are hot.

Servings: 9 | Serving Size: 2 mini boats

Calories 145 | Fat 0g | Carbohydrates 4g | Protein 13g

Preparation Time: 15 minutes | Cooking Time: 10 minutes

# Caprese Grilled Chicken with Balsamic Reduction

- 6 grilled boneless, skinless chicken breasts
- ¼ cup balsamic vinegar
- 1 Tbs butter
- 6 slices mozzarella cheese
- 6 slices tomato
- 6 large basil leaves

- Grill the chicken over medium high heat for 5-6 minutes per side, or until cooked through.
- Meanwhile, heat the vinegar in a pan over medium high heat. Reduce by half.
- Stir in the butter and then set aside.
- Top the chicken with the cheese, basil and tomato.
- Drizzle the balsamic reduction over the top and serve immediately.

Servings: 6 | Serving Size: 6.4 oz

Calories 244 | Fat 10g | Carbohydrates 3g | Protein 34g

Preparation Time: 5 minutes | Cooking Time: 25 minutes

# Cheesy Broccoli, Chicken and Rice Bowls

- 1.5 lbs boneless skinless chicken breasts
- Kosher salt and freshly-cracked black pepper
- 2 Tbs olive oil, divided
- 2 heads broccoli, cut into bite-sized florets
- 3 cups cooked rice or quinoa
- extra shredded cheddar cheese, for topping
- Cheddar Cheese Sauce:
- 1 Tbs butter
- 2 cloves garlic, pressed or minced
- 2 Tbs cream cheese
- 1/2 cup chicken or vegetable stock
- 1/2 cup warmed milk
- ¼ tsp pepper
- ⅛ tsp salt
- 1 cup (4 ounces) shredded sharp cheddar cheese

- Season the chicken with salt and pepper.
- Heat 1 Tbs of oil in a large skillet over medium high heat and cook the chicken for 4-5 minutes per side, or until cooked through.
- Remove and let the chicken cool slightly before cutting into bite sized pieces.
- Heat the remaining tablespoon of oil in the pan and sauté the broccoli for 4-5 minutes, or until just tender. Season with salt and pepper and set aside.
- Sauté the garlic in the butter for the cheese sauce for 1-2 minutes.
- Stir in the cream cheese until melted and then whisk in the stock, milk, pepper and salt. Whisk until smooth.
- Stir in the cheese and whisk until melted and thick.
- Combine the chicken and broccoli with the cheese sauce and serve over rice.

Servings: 6 | Serving Size: 15.1 oz

Calories 513 | Fat 21g | Carbohydrates 32g | Protein 49g

Preparation Time: 10 minutes | Cooking Time: 20 minutes

# Chicken and Green Chile Egg Muffins

- 11 large eggs
- 1 4-ounce can of green chiles
- 1/2 tsp salt
- 1 pinch black pepper
- 1/4 cup mozzarella cheese, shredded
- 1/4 cup cilantro, chopped
- 1/2 cup cooked and shredded chicken

- Preheat the oven to 375 degrees F. Line a muffin pan with paper liners and set aside.
- Whisk together the eggs, chilies, salt, pepper, mozzarella cheese and cilantro.
- Evenly divide the mixture into the prepared pan.
- Top with the shredded chicken.
- Bake for 20 minutes, then let rest for 5 minutes before serving.

Servings: 8 | Serving Size: 3.7 oz

Calories 115 | Fat 7g | Carbohydrates 1g | Protein 10g

Preparation Time: 10 minutes | Cooking Time: 20 minutes

# Chicken and Potatoes with Garlic Parmesan Cream Sauce

- 6 bone-in, skin-on chicken thighs
- 1 Tbs Italian seasoning
- Kosher salt and freshly ground black pepper, to taste
- 3 Tbs unsalted butter, divided
- 3 cups baby spinach, roughly chopped
- 16 oz baby Dutch potatoes, halved*
- 2 Tbs chopped fresh parsley leaves
- For the garlic parmesan cream sauce
- 1/4 cup unsalted butter
- 4 cloves garlic, minced
- 2 Tbs cream cheese
- ½ cup chicken broth
- 1 tsp dried thyme
- 1/2 tsp dried basil
- 1/2 cup half and half
- 1/2 cup freshly grated Parmesan
- Kosher salt and freshly ground black pepper, to taste

- Preheat the oven to 400 degrees F and lightly grease a 9x13-inch baking dish.
- Season the chicken with Italian seasoning, salt and pepper.
- Sear the chicken for 2-3 minutes per side in 2 Tbs of butter in a large skillet.
- Remove and set aside.
- Add the remaining butter into the skillet and cook the spinach for 2 minutes, or until wilted.
- Melt the butter in a skillet and sauté the garlic for 1-2 minutes.
- Melt the cream cheese and then stir in the chicken broth, thyme and basil. Cook for 1-2 minutes.
- Stir in the half and half and cheese until thickened, about 2 minutes.
- Season to taste with salt and pepper.
- Place the chicken in the baking dish and top with the potatoes, spinach and then pour the cream sauce over the top.
- Bake for 25-30 minutes, or until cooked through.
- Garnish with parsley before serving.

Servings: 6 | Serving Size: 11.9 oz

Calories 382 | Fat 23g | Carbohydrates 24g | Protein 22g

Preparation Time: 10 minutes | Cooking Time: 40 minutes

# Chicken and Veggies

- 2 medium chicken breasts, boneless skinless cut into ½ inch pieces
- 1 cup broccoli florets, frozen or fresh
- 1 small red onion, chopped
- 1 cup grape or plum tomatoes
- 1 medium zucchini, chopped
- 2 cloves garlic minced
- 1 Tbs italian seasoning
- 1 tsp salt
- ½ tsp black pepper (optional)
- ½ tsp red pepper flakes (optional)
- ½ tsp paprika
- 2 Tbs olive oil
- 2 cups brown rice, cooked

- Preheat the oven to 450 degrees F and line a baking sheet with aluminum foil.
- Combine the chicken and veggies in the prepared pan and drizzle on the olive oil, then sprinkle on the spices and garlic. Toss gently to combine.
- Bake for 15-20 minutes, or until the chicken is tender and the vegetables are charred.
- Serve with rice, if desired.

Servings: 4 | Serving Size: 10.4 oz

Calories 278 | Fat 10g | Carbohydrates 31g | Protein 18g

Preparation Time: 10 minutes | Cooking Time: 20 minutes

# Chicken Carnitas Burrito Bowls

- 1 lb boneless chicken breasts
- 1 Tbs olive oil
- Salt and ground fresh black pepper
- 3 garlic cloves, minced
- 1 medium sweet potato, peeled and diced
- ½ cup chicken broth or water
- ½ lb fresh asparagus (the spears should be cut at a diagonal in 1 and 2 inch pieces)
- ½ tsp fine sea salt
- ½ tsp freshly ground black pepper
- ½ tsp crushed red pepper
- For the Carnitas
- 1 lb boneless skinless chicken breast
- 3 Tbs olive oil, divided
- 1 Tbs minced garlic
- 1-2 cups chicken broth
- 1 Tbs orange juice
- 1/3 cup lime juice
- 3 tsp ground cumin
- 2 tsp smoked paprika
- salt and pepper, to taste
- 1/4 cup green chiles
- For the Street Corn
- 1 can yellow sweet corn, drained
- 2 Tbs lime juice
- 1/2 Tbs apple cider vinegar
- 2 Tbs chopped cilantro, fresh
- 1/3 cup red onion, finely chopped
- 1/3 cup cotija cheese, crumbled
- 1/2 tsp paprika
- salt and pepper, to taste
- 2 cups brown rice, cooked
- Other Ingredients
- 1 cup Black beans
- 4 cups romaine lettuce, shredded
- Lime wedges

- Cut the chicken into 1-inch pieces and season liberally with salt and pepper.
- Heat the olive oil in a skillet over medium heat and brown the chicken and garlic in the oil for 7-10 minutes, or until the chicken is cooked through.
- Remove the chicken and add the sweet potato and chicken broth to the pan.
- Cook for 7-10 minutes, or until the sweet potato is tender.
- Add the asparagus and continue to cook for another 4-5 minutes.
- Return the chicken to the pan and cook for 1-2 minutes, or until the chicken is hot again.
- Season to taste with salt, pepper and crushed red pepper before serving.
- Brown the chicken and garlic in the oil and then place in a slow cooker with 1-2 cups chicken broth.
- Cook on low for 6-8 hours.
- Remove the meat and shred the meat.
- Return the meat to the slow cooker and reserve about ¼ cup of the juice. Discard the remaining juice.
- Add the remaining carnitas ingredients to the slow cooker and mix well. Cover and cook on low until serving.
- Meanwhile, mix together the street corn ingredients and set aside.

- Serve the meat with the rice, street corn and black beans.
- Garnish with lime and additional cotija.

Servings: 4 | Serving Size: 20.6 oz

Calories 491 | Fat 18g | Carbohydrates 66g | Protein 22g

Preparation Time: 10 minutes | Cooking Time: 8 hours

# Chicken Posole

- Sauce Ingredients
- 8 tomatillos
- 3 serrano chilies (can be reduced or added, depending on the heat you want your soup to be)
- 2 tomatoes
- 1 garlic clove
- 5 sprigs of cilantro
- ¼ tsp of salt, or to taste
- pinch of oregano
- pinch of cumin
- Soup Ingredients
- 3 chicken breast
- ½ chopped yellow onion
- 2 chopped garlic cloves
- 2 tsp of salt
- 29 oz of white hominy, drained & rinsed
- 32 oz of low sodium chicken stock

- Preheat the oven to 400 degrees F.
- Brush the chilies and tomatoes with olive oil and roast for 30 minutes.
- Set aside and allow to cool.
- Boil the tomatillos (with the husk removed) for 5 minutes.
- Drain and then combine with the roasted tomatoes, chilies, cilantro, salt, cumin and oregano. Puree.
- Meanwhile, cover the chicken with water in a heavy stockpot and add the onion, garlic and salt.
- Bring to a boil, then reduce heat to a simmer.
- Cook for 10 minutes, then turn off heat and let sit for 15-20 minutes.
- Shred the chicken.
- Return the chicken to the pot.
- Add the tomatillo sauce to the pot.
- Add the broth and hominy, then bring to a boil.
- Reduce heat to simmer for 30 minutes.
- Serve hot with avocado, cilantro, onion or lime, if desired.

Servings: 8 | Serving Size: 1 cup

Calories 172 | Fat 0g | Carbohydrates 19g | Protein 17g

Preparation Time: 20 minutes | Cooking Time: 1 hour

*Note: this soup can also be cooked on high in a slow cooker for 2 hours instead of cooked for 30 minutes on the stove.

# Creamy Chicken and Mushroom Ragout

- 1.25 lbs chicken breast filets (about two filets), cut into strips, then halved
- 1 Tbs extra-virgin olive oil, divided
- 1/4 tsp kosher or sea salt, divided
- 1/4 tsp black pepper, divided
- 1 cup cleaned and sliced baby bella mushrooms
- 1/4 cup chopped white onion
- 1 clove garlic, minced
- 1/2 cup dry white chicken or vegetable stock or chicken broth
- 1 (14 ounce) can coconut milk
- 6 whole sprigs fresh thyme
- Small pinch nutmeg

- Season the chicken with salt and pepper.
- Heat 2 tsp of oil in a skillet over medium heat.
- Cook the chicken for 8 minutes per side, or until cooked through. Set aside.
- Add the remaining oil and sauté the mushrooms, thyme and onions for 5-8 minutes, or until the onions have softened.
- Add the garlic and cook for another 30 seconds.
- Add the chicken or vegetable stock (or broth) and deglaze the pan. Cook for 4-5 minutes, or until about half of the liquid has evaporated.
- Add the coconut milk and nutmeg and mix well.
- Return the chicken to the pan and season with salt and pepper.
- Cook for 3-5 minutes or until cooked through. If desired, cook for a few more minutes to thicken slightly.
- Remove the thyme and serve with side of choice (rice, spaghetti squash, quinoa, etc.).

Servings: 6 | Serving Size: 1 cup

Calories 256 | Fat 0g | Carbohydrates 4g | Protein 19g

Preparation Time: 10 minutes | Cooking Time: 30 minutes

# Creamy Sun-dried Tomato Chicken

- 1 Tbs salt
- 1 tsp Freshly Ground Pepper
- 8 Chicken thighs (bone-in, skin removed)
- 3 Tbs Extra Virgin Olive Oil divided
- 1 Yellow Onion Sliced thinly
- 3/4 cup Sliced Sun-dried Tomatoes (not packed in oil)
- 1 Tbs Garlic minced
- 1 tsp Italian Seasoning (oregano, thyme, parsley)
- large pinch Red Pepper Flakes
- 13.5 oz can Coconut Milk
- 1 cup Chicken Stock or Broth
- Basil shredded, to top

- Preheat the oven to 400 degrees F.
- Season the chicken on all sides with salt and pepper.
- Fry the chicken, in an oven safe skillet, in the olive oil for 2-3 minutes, or until browned on all sides.
- Set aside.
- Add a little more oil to the pan and sauté the onion for 2 minutes.
- Add the tomatoes, garlic, Italian seasoning and red pepper and cook for 30 seconds.
- Stir in the coconut milk and chicken broth and bring the mixture ot a boil.
- Place the chicken back into the sauce and spoon some sauce on top.
- Cover and bake for 45 minutes.
- Reduce heat to 300 degrees F and cook for another 20 minutes.
- Garnish with basil before serving.

Servings: 8 | Serving Size: 5.9 oz

Calories 162 | Fat 8g | Carbohydrates 7g | Protein 16g

Preparation Time: 15 minutes | Cooking Time: 1 hour and 15 minutes

# Crock Pot Thai Chicken Curry

- 2 cups water
- 2-4 Tbs Thai red curry paste, or to taste
- 1 Tbs soy sauce
- 1 Tbs minced ginger
- 2 tsp fish sauce
- 3 garlic cloves, minced
- 1 lb boneless, skinless chicken thighs, cut into 2-3 pieces
- 1 large kabocha, cut into 1 – inch cubes (or 1 small butternut squash)
- 1 medium yellow onion, chopped
- 1-2 chili peppers, optional
- 1 14 oz can coconut milk
- 1 large bunch of kale, torn into small pieces (roughly 2 packed cups)
- Cilantro and lime wedges for serving

- Combine all ingredients, except the coconut milk and kale in a slow cooker and mix well.
- Cook on high for 4 hours and then stir in the coconut milk and kale.
- Mix well and cook on high for another 15-20 minutes, or until hot through and the kale has wilted.
- Season to taste with salt and pepper and serve with cilantro and lime wedges.

Servings: 4 | Serving Size: 18.4 oz

Calories 436 | Fat 28g | Carbohydrates 24g | Protein 28g

Preparation Time: 10 minutes | Cooking Time: 4 hours

*Note: make sure the red curry paste does not contain sugar.

# Fajita Stuffed Chicken

- 4 chicken breasts
- 2 Tbs olive oil
- 2 Tbs taco seasoning
- 1/2 each red, yellow and green pepper, diced
- 1 small red onion, diced
- 1/2 cup shredded cheese
- Cilantro (optional for garnish)
- Salsa and sour cream

- Roasted sweet potatoes (optional side)
- 1 Tbs olive oil
- 3 sweet potatoes, cut into 1-inch pieces
- 2 tsp chili powder
- 2 tsp paprika
- 2 tsp garlic powder
- 1 tsp salt

- Preheat the oven to 450 degrees F.
- Coat the sweet potatoes in olive oil and the spices and roast in a baking dish or sheet pan for 25-30 minutes, or until tender.
- Meanwhile, make a slit in the side of each chicken breast.
- Combine the bell peppers and onions and stuff into the slit.
- Grill the chicken for 15 minutes on medium high.
- Sprinkle on the cheese and grill for another 5 minutes, or until the cheese is melted.
- Serve with the sweet potatoes and other toppings of choice.

Servings: 4 | Serving Size: 16.9 oz

Calories 591 | Fat 18g | Carbohydrates 45g | Protein 60g

Preparation Time: 15 minutes | Cooking Time: 30 minutes

*Note: if unable to find a sugar free taco seasoning, use the following recipe: 2 teaspoons Chili Powder

1-1/2 teaspoon Ground Cumin; 1/2 teaspoon Paprika; 1/2 teaspoon Crushed Red Pepper; 1/2 teaspoon Salt; 1/4 teaspoon Garlic Powder; 1/4 teaspoon Onion Powder; 1/4 teaspoon Dried Oregano; 1/4 teaspoon Black Pepper

# Grilled Lemon Rosemary Chicken

- 2 lbs chicken breast fillets
- ¼ cup olive oil
- 3 cloves garlic, minced
- zest from one lemon
- juice from one lemon (about ¼ cup)
- ¾ tsp salt
- ¼ tsp pepper
- 2 large sprigs rosemary

- Combine all ingredients in a bag and mix well.
- Refrigerate for 3 hours to allow the chicken to marinate.
- Grill over medium heat for 3-4 minutes per side, or until cooked through.
- Serve hot.

Servings: 8 | Serving Size: 4.6 oz

Calories 251 | Fat 11g | Carbohydrates 1g | Protein 35g

Preparation Time: 5 minutes | Cooking Time: 15 minutes | Inactive Time: 3 hours

# Jalapeño Turkey Burgers

- 1 lb ground turkey
- 1/2-3/4 of one jalapeño pepper, minced
- 1 medium size shallot, peeled and minced
- zest and of one lime, and 2 teaspoon lime juice
- 2 Tbs chopped cilantro
- 1 tsp paprika
- 1 tsp cumin
- 1/2 a teaspoon sea salt
- 1/2 tsp black pepper
- guacamole
- pico de gallo

- Combine all ingredients in a bowl and mix well.
- Form into 4 patties.
- Preheat a skillet on medium heat and add a little olive oil.
- Cook the patties for 5 minutes per side, or until cooked through.
- Serve with guacamole, pico de gallo or toppings of choice.

Servings: 4 | Serving Size: 8 oz

Calories 248 | Fat 9g | Carbohydrates 19g | Protein 25g

Preparation Time: 10 minutes | Cooking Time: 10 minutes

# Italian Skillet Chicken with Tomatoes and Mushrooms

- 4 large chicken cutlets (boneless skinless chicken breasts cut into 1/4-inch thin cutlets)
- 1 Tbs dried oregano, divided
- 1 tsp salt, divided
- 1 tsp black pepper, divided
- 2-3 Tbs olive oil
- 8 oz Baby Bella mushrooms, cleaned, trimmed, and sliced
- 14 oz grape tomatoes, halved
- 2 Tbs chopped fresh garlic
- 1/2 cup chicken or vegetable stock
- 1 Tbs freshly squeezed lemon juice (juice of 1/2 lemon)
- 3/4 cup chicken broth
- Handful baby spinach (optional)

- Season the chicken on both sides with half of the oregano, salt and pepper.
- Heat 2 Tbs of oil in a heavy skillet and brown the chicken on both sides for 3 minutes.
- Remove the chicken and set aside.
- Sauté the mushrooms in the same skillet, add another tablespoon of oil if needed.
- Add the tomatoes, garlic and remaining oregano, salt and pepper.
- Cook for another 3 minutes.
- Deglaze the pan with the chicken or vegetable stock and then stir in the chicken broth and lemon juice.
- Bring the liquid to a boil and then return the chicken to the pan.
- Reduce heat to medium and simmer for 8-10 minutes, or until the chicken is fully cooked and the liquid is reduced to desired consistency.

Serve with rice or quinoa, if desired.

Servings: 4 | Serving Size: 14.8 oz

Calories 278 | Fat 11g | Carbohydrates 12g | Protein 34g

Preparation Time: 10 minutes | Cooking Time: 20 minutes

# Italian Style Stuffed Zucchini Boats

- 6 large zucchini
- olive oil
- kosher salt
- freshly ground black pepper
- 1/4 tsp garlic powder
- 1 small yellow onion, diced
- 2 cloves garlic, minced
- 1 lb ground turkey
- 1 28 oz can crushed tomatoes
- 4 oz mozzerella cheese, shredded
- 1 oz freshly grated parmesan cheese
- flat leaf parsley for garnish

- Preheat the oven to 425 degrees F and lightly grease a 9x13-inch baking dish with cooking spray.
- Slice the zucchini in half lengthwise and then scoop out the seeds.
- Brush with olive oil and season with salt, pepper and garlic powder.
- Roast in the prepared dish for 20 minutes, or until it begins to soften.
- Meanwhile, sauté the onions and garlic in a ½ Tbs of olive oil over medium high heat in a large skillet.
- Cook for 3-4 minutes, then add the ground turkey and brown.
- Add the tomatoes and bring to a boil.
- Reduce heat to medium and then let simmer until the zucchini are done.
- Stir in ½ tsp salt and pepper to taste.
- Fill the zucchini boats with the meat mixture and sprinkle on shredded cheese.
- Bake until the cheese is melted, about 3-5 minutes.
- Serve hot, garnished with parmesan cheese and parsley.

Servings: 6 | Serving Size: 16.3 oz

Calories 298 | Fat 17g | Carbohydrates 14g | Protein 25g

Preparation Time: 5 minutes | Cooking Time: 25 minutes

# Lemon Rosemary Chicken

- 1/4 cup olive oil
- 4 chicken breasts
- 1 1/2 sweet potatoes, cubed
- 1 large lemon, squeezed
- 1 large lemon, sliced
- 2 Tbs rosemary
- 5 garlic cloves, crushed
- Salt and pepper, to taste

- Preheat the oven to 400 degrees F.
- Grease an oven safe skillet with oil and heat over medium high heat.
- Season the chicken with salt and pepper on both sides and then brown the chicken and sweet potatoes for 4-5 minutes per side or until the chicken is browned.
- Add the lemon, rosemary and garlic and place the sliced lemons on top.
- Bake for 30-35 minutes, or until the chicken is cooked through.
- Serve.

Servings: 4 | Serving Size: 16.1 oz

Calories 621 | Fat 20g | Carbohydrates 52g | Protein 56g

Preparation Time: 5 minutes | Cooking Time: 45 minutes

# Market Chicken Skillet

- 1 1/2 lbs boneless skinless chicken breast, cubed
- 1 small fennel bulb, cored and sliced thin
- 1 orange bell pepper, seeded and sliced
- 2 zucchini, halved and sliced
- 3 cups chopped fresh kale
- 1 pint fresh grape or cherry tomatoes
- 1 1/4 cups fresh corn kernels (optional)
- 2 garlic cloves, minced
- 2-3 tablespoons golden balsamic vinegar
- 2 Tbs olive oil
- 1 Tbs dried Italian Seasoning
- Salt and pepper

- Heat a large skillet over medium high heat with 1 Tbs of oil.
- Sear the fennel and pepper until charred on all sides and then set aside.
- Sear the zucchini for 1-2 minutes per side, or until just browned. Set aside.
- Season the chicken with salt, pepper and Italian seasoning.
- Add the remaining oil to the skillet and cook the chicken for 2 minutes per side.
- Add the garlic, kale and tomatoes and cook for another 2 minutes.
- Return all the vegetables to the pan and the corn, vinegar and water.
- Mix well and continue to cook until warmed through and the chicken is completely cooked.
- Season to taste with salt and pepper.

Servings: 6 | Serving Size: 12.2 oz

Calories 312 | Fat 10g | Carbohydrates 17g | Protein 39g

Preparation Time: 10 minutes | Cooking Time: 15 minutes

# One Pot Chicken & Rice Dinner

- 2 cups cooked basmati rice
- ¼ cup water
- 1/4 cup lite (low sodium) soy sauce, optional Tamari
- 1/2 cup lemon juice (from 1 lemon)
- 2-3 tablespoons extra-virgin olive oil
- 1 lb chicken white meat, strips
- 1 can baby corn
- 1/2 tsp salt
- 1/4 tsp ground pepper
- 2 Tbs chives, finely chopped

- Combine the water, soy sauce and lemon in a small bowl. Mix well.
- Heat 2 Tbs olive oil and cook the chicken over medium high heat in a skillet until cooked through.
- Add the soy mixture and baby corn. Simmer for 15 minutes to reduce the sauce.
- Add in the remaining ingredients, except chives, and season to taste.
- Continue to cook for 4-5 minutes, or until the rice is heated through.
- Garnish with chives and serve.

Servings: 4 | Serving Size: 9.6 oz

Calories 177 | Fat 1g | Carbohydrates 31g | Protein 11g

Preparation Time: 10 minutes | Cooking Time: 25 minutes

# One Pot Thai Quinoa Bowl with Chicken and Spicy Peanut Sauce

- 1 Tbs olive oil
- 1 small red onion, chopped
- 3 garlic cloves, minced
- 2 cups broccoli, chopped
- 2 cups sliced red cabbage
- 2 cups julienned carrots
- 1 cup uncooked quinoa, rinsed and drained
- 2 1/2 cups chicken stock
- 2 tsp ground ginger
- 1 1/2 tsp sea salt
- 1 1/2 tsp pepper
- 2 cups frozen edamame, thawed
- 2 cups precooked, chopped chicken

- Peanut Sauce:
- 1/4 cup peanut butter
- 3 Tbs water
- 3 Tbs rice vinegar
- 1 Tbs soy sauce
- 1/8 tsp sesame oil
- 1/4 tsp red pepper flakes
- 1/4 tsp ground ginger
- For Garnish:
- Handful Cilantro
- 1/4 cup Chopped Peanuts

- Sauté the onion in the olive oil over medium heat for 4-5 minutes.
- Add the garlic and cook for another 30 seconds.
- Stir in the broccoli, cabbage and carrots and cook for 1 minute.
- Mix in the quinoa, stock, ginger, salt and pepper and cook, covered, for 20 minutes.
- Stir in the edamame and chicken and cook for another 1-2 minutes, or until the chicken is cooked through.
- While the quinoa is cooking, combine the peanut sauce ingredients and puree.
- Serve the quinoa topped with the peanut sauce and garnished with cilantro and chopped peanuts.

Servings: 6 | Serving Size: 13.3 oz

Calories 425 | Fat 18g | Carbohydrates 39g | Protein 33g

Preparation Time: 10 minutes | Cooking Time: 40 minutes

*Note: Be sure to use a natural peanut butter without any sugar added. If necessary, process 1 cup of roasted peanuts in a food processor for 2-3 minutes until peanut butter forms. If needed, add a teaspoon or two of oil until desired consistency is reached. (This works with almonds and cashews as well). The nut butter will last for up to one month in the refrigerator.

# One-Pot Italian Chicken & Quinoa

- 8 boneless, skinless chicken thighs, trimmed
- 1 tsp dried oregano
- 1/2 tsp salt
- 1/2 tsp ground pepper
- 2 1/2 tsp olive oil, divided
- 1/2 onion, chopped
- 3 carrots, cut into half-circles
- 3 garlic cloves, minced
- 1 (28 oz.) can crushed tomatoes
- 1 cup water
- 1 cup quinoa
- 1/4 cup minced flat-leaf parsley
- 5 basil leaves, thinly sliced

- Combine the chicken, oregano, salt and pepper in a bowl and mix well to coat the chicken with the spices.
- Heat 1 ½ tsp of oil in a large skillet over medium high and cook the chicken for 2 minutes per side. Remove the chicken.
- Heat the remaining oil over medium and sauté the onions and carrots for 4-5 minutes.
- Stir in the tomatoes, water and quinoa and bring to a boil.
- Reduce heat and simmer, covered, for 15 minutes.
- Add the chicken back to the pan and continue to cook for 15 minutes, or until the liquid is absorbed and the chicken is cooked through.
- Remove from the heat and let sit, uncovered, for 5 minutes.
- Stir in the parsley and basil before serving.

Servings: 6 | Serving Size: 10.5 oz

Calories 278 | Fat 8g | Carbohydrates 28g | Protein 24g

Preparation Time: 10 minutes | Cooking Time: 40 minutes

# Ragu Stuffed Portobello Mushrooms

- 1 ¼ tsp olive oil
- ½ yellow onion
- ½ large carrot, diced
- ½ large celery stalk, diced
- 2 garlic cloves, minced
- ¾ tsp dried oregano
- ¾ lb ground turkey
- 14 oz crushed tomatoes
- ¼ tsp + 1/8 tsp salt, or to taste
- 3 Tbs minced flat-leaf parsley
- 3 basil leaves, thinly sliced
- 4 large portabella mushrooms
- 2 tsp olive oil
- 1/8 tsp salt
- 1/8 tsp ground pepper
- 6 Tbs grated part skim mozzarella cheese

- Preheat the oven to 425 degrees F.
- Remove the stems and gills from each mushroom.
- Brush with olive oil and season with salt and pepper.
- Place in a single layer in a baking dish and bake for 12-15 minutes, or until tender.
- Meanwhile, heat the oil in a large skillet over medium heat and sauté the onion, carrots and celery.
- Cook for 7-8 minutes, or until tender.
- Increase heat to medium high and cook the ground turkey until cooked through, about 10 minutes. Be sure to break up the meat with a spoon during the cooking so that no large pieces remain.
- Add the tomatoes and salt and bring to a boil.
- Simmer for 10 minutes, then stir in the parsley and basil. Season to taste with additional salt and pepper.
- Reduce the oven temperature to 375 degrees F.
- Remove any liquid from the mushrooms and fill with about a ½ cup of the sauce.
- Sprinkle on the cheese and bake for 8-10 minutes, or until the cheese is melted and the mushrooms are tender.

Servings: 4 | Serving Size: 14 oz

Calories 274 | Fat 14g | Carbohydrates 15g | Protein 25g

Preparation Time: 10 minutes | Cooking Time: 50 minutes

# Roasted Chicken and Veggies

- 2 medium chicken breasts, chopped
- 1 cup bell pepper, any color, chopped
- ½ onion, chopped
- 1 zucchini, chopped
- 1 cup broccoli florets
- ½ cup tomatoes, chopped or plum/grape
- 2 Tbs olive oil
- ½ tsp salt
- ½ tsp black pepper
- 1 tsp Italian seasoning
- ¼ tsp paprika (optional)

- Preheat the oven to 500 degrees F.
- Combine the chicken and vegetables on a sheet pan or in a roasting dish.
- Drizzle on the olive oil and season with the spices. Mix well.
- Bake for 15 minutes, or until the chicken is cooked through and the vegetables are lightly charred.
- Serve immediately.

Servings: 2 | Serving Size: 12.7 oz

Calories 327 | Fat 17g | Carbohydrates 13g | Protein 30g

Preparation Time: 5 minutes | Cooking Time: 15 minutes

# Sausage and Veggies

- 1 lbs Dutch Yellow Potatoes
- ¾ lbs pound green beans
- 4 links organic, sugar free chicken apple sausage
- 6 Tbs olive oil
- 8 baby carrots
- 6 oz Cherry Tomatoes
- 4 baby cauliflower
- 1 Bell Pepper, Sliced

- Preheat the oven to 400 degrees F and line a large baking pan with aluminum foil.
- Combine the vegetables, except the tomatoes, and sausage to the pan.
- Bake for 15 minutes, then stir.
- Add the tomatoes and cook for another 20 minutes, or until the vegetables are tender and the sausage is browned.
- Serve hot.

Servings: 4 | Serving Size: 19.7 oz

Calories 477 | Fat 28g | Carbohydrates 39g | Protein 21g

Preparation Time: 10 minutes | Cooking Time: 25 minutes

# Shredded Chicken Primavera Bowl

- 2 Tbs olive oil
- 1 small onion, sliced
- 3 cloves garlic, minced
- 1 red bell pepper, sliced
- 1 yellow bell pepper, sliced
- 1 small carrot, thinly sliced
- 1 tsp thyme leaves
- 2 cups baby spinach leaves
- 1 cup cooked and shredded chicken breast
- Juice of 1 lemon
- 1/2 cup alfalfa sprouts
- Salt and pepper

- Sauté the onion and garlic in oil over medium heat until tender, about 5 minutes.
- Add the peppers and carrots and sauté for another 3-4 minutes, or until beginning to get tender.
- Season with the thyme, salt and pepper and mix well.
- Stir in the chicken and spinach and cook for 2-3 minutes, or until the spinach is wilted and the chicken heated through.
- Stir in the lemon juice and garnish with the alfalfa sprouts before serving.

Servings: 2 | Serving Size: 1 cup

Calories 322 | Fat 0g | Carbohydrates 15g | Protein 27g

Preparation Time: 5 minutes | Cooking Time: 15 minutes

# Slow Cooker Herb Crusted Turkey Breast

- 2 1/2 lb turkey breast
- 1 Tbs garlic powder
- 1 Tbs poultry seasoning
- 1 tsp dried thyme
- 1/4 tsp black pepper
- 1 Tbs onion powder

- Combine all spices in a small bowl.
- Rub the spices on the turkey breast and then cook in a slow cooker, with no additional liquid, for 4-5 hours on low, or until cooked through.

Servings: 6 | Serving Size: 6.8 oz

Calories 209 | Fat 3g | Carbohydrates 11g | Protein 33g

Preparation Time: 5 minutes | Cooking Time: 5 hours

# Slow Cooker Enchilada Bake

- 2 half chicken breasts, with bone and skin
- 1 (16 ounce) jar red enchilada sauce
- 1 (4 ounce) can green chile peppers
- 1/2 tsp garlic powder
- 1 tsp cumin
- 1 tsp chili powder
- 1/2 tsp black pepper
- 1 1/2 cups shredded cheddar cheese
- 1 (8 oz.) container sour cream

- Preheat the oven to 350 degrees F. Bake the chicken in a covered dish for 45 minutes, or until cooked through.
- Cool slightly and remove the bone and skin. Discard and then shred the chicken.
- Combine the chicken, garlic powder, cumin, chili powder, pepper and salt.
- Stir in the green chile peppers, sauce, sour cream and 1 cup of cheese.
- Place the enchilada mixture into the slow cooker and cook for 3-4 hours on low, or until bubbly.
- Serve with the remaining cheese, diced tomatoes, shredded lettuce and a side of rice, if desired.

Servings: 6 | Serving Size: 6.1 oz

Calories 289 | Fat 20g | Carbohydrates 7g | Protein 20g

Preparation Time: 50 minutes | Cooking Time: 4 hours

*Note: Precooked, shredded chicken can also be used in place of cooking the chicken. Use 1 pound and 3 oz of cooked, shredded chicken.

# Slow Cooker Indian Chicken and Rice

- 3 chicken breasts (2 lbs), skinless, boneless, cut into 1" strips
- 1 cup long grain brown rice (uncooked)
- 1/2 cup Greek Yogurt, low fat, plain
- 2 cups chicken broth, fat free, low sodium
- 1 (4 oz.) can Green Chile Peppers, drained and diced
- 1/4 tsp ginger
- 1/4 tsp cinnamon
- 1/4 tsp cloves
- 1/4 tsp turmeric
- 1/2 tsp cayenne pepper
- 1 tsp black pepper
- 1 tsp chili powder
- 1 tsp coriander
- 1 tsp curry
- 1 tsp paprika
- Salt to taste
- 1 Bay Leaf
- 4 Tbs fresh mint leaves
- 1 Tbs Extra Virgin olive oil
- 1 medium onion, cut into thin rings
- 2 cloves garlic, minced

- Sauté the onion and garlic in 1 Tbs of oil over medium high heat. Cook for 5 minutes, or until the onion is tender.
- Reserve a little mint (about 2 Tbs) and a few onion rings for garnish.
- Combine the onion, garlic, spices and herbs, yogurt, chicken broth and chicken strips. Mix well and then cover and refrigerate for 1-2 hours.
- Place the rice on the bottom of the slow cooker and top with the chicken mixture.
- Cook on high for 3-4 hours or low for 5-6 hours.
- Check after 2 hours to see if additional liquid is needed. If a little more is needed, add another ½ cup of chicken broth.
- Once the chicken is cooked through and the rice is tender, remove the bay leaf and garnish with the reserved mint and onion rings.

Servings: 6 | Serving Size: 3/4 cup

Calories 254 | Fat 0g | Carbohydrates 34g | Protein 18g

Preparation Time: 10 minutes | Cooking Time: 6 hours

# Slow Cooker Stuffed Peppers

- 2/3 cup long grain white rice
- 1 1/2 lbs ground turkey
- 1 small onion
- 2 cloves garlic
- 1/2 Tbs italian seasoning
- 1/2 tsp chili flakes
- 28 oz can diced tomatoes, undrained
- 1 Tbs tomato paste
- 1 Tbs soy sauce
- 1 1/2 cups shredded cheddar cheese, divided
- 1 cup chicken broth
- 6 bell peppers (red, green, yellow or orange)

- Bring 1 ½ cups of water to a boil and then stir in the rice.
- Reduce heat and cook for 15-18 minutes, or until the water is gone but the rice is not quite done.
- Meanwhile, brown the turkey, onion and garlic in a large skillet over medium heat until the turkey is cooked through.
- Stir in 2/3 of the tomatoes, seasoning, chili flakes, tomato paste and soy sauce until well combined.
- Stir in the rice.
- Slice the tops off the peppers and place in the bottom of a slow cooker.
- Fill each pepper halfway with the rice mixture.
- Sprinkle on a ¼ cup of cheese and then top with the remaining rice mixture.
- Top the peppers with the remaining tomatoes and broth.
- Cook on high for 3 hours, or until tender.
- Rest for 5 minutes before sprinkling on the remaining cheese and serving.

Servings: 6 | Serving Size: 17.9 oz

Calories 395 | Fat 21g | Carbohydrates 21g | Protein 34g

Preparation Time: 25 minutes | Cooking Time: 3 hours

# Taco Potatoes

- 4 medium russet potatoes
- 1 lb ground turkey
- 1 oz taco seasoning
- TOPPINGS
- shredded lettuce
- cheddar cheese
- sour cream
- salsa
- guacamole
- green onion

- Preheat the oven to 400 degrees F. Poke at least 2-3 holes in each potato with a knife or fork and wrap in foil.
- Bake for 1 hour and then set aside to cool slightly before serving.
- Meanwhile, in a skillet brown the ground turkey.
- Season the meat with the taco seasoning and a ¼ cup water. Simmer for 10 minutes.
- Cut a slit in the top of each potato and fill with the ground turkey.
- Top with favorite toppings before serving.

Servings: 4 | Serving Size: 8.6 oz

Calories 316 | Fat 9g | Carbohydrates 34g | Protein 26g

Preparation Time: 15 minutes | Cooking Time: 1 hour

*Note: if unable to find a sugar free taco seasoning, use the following recipe: 2 teaspoons Chili Powder

1-1/2 teaspoon Ground Cumin; 1/2 teaspoon Paprika; 1/2 teaspoon Crushed Red Pepper; 1/2 teaspoon Salt; 1/4 teaspoon Garlic Powder; 1/4 teaspoon Onion Powder; 1/4 teaspoon Dried Oregano; 1/4 teaspoon Black Pepper

The toppings are not included in the nutrition information or serving size.

# Thai Chicken Lettuce Cups

- 1 1/2 Tbs cooking oil
- 1/2 lb ground chicken breast
- 2 shallots, diced
- 1/4 red onion, diced
- 1 clove garlic, very finely minced
- Minced fresh chiles, Jalapeño or Fresno (amount up to you)
- 1 Tbs fish sauce
- 1/2 lime, juiced
- 1 tsp low-sodium soy sauce
- 1 head iceberg lettuce, leaves separated into "cups"
- 1 handful of cilantro and/or mint, cut into chiffonade

- Heat 1 Tbs of oil in a large pan or wok over high heat and cook the chicken for 3 minutes, or until browned.
- Add the remaining oil to the pan and sauté the shallots, garlic, red onion and chilies for 30 seconds.
- Add the fish sauce, lime juice and soy sauce.
- Serve in the lettuce cups and garnished with the fresh herbs.

Servings: 6 | Serving Size: 10.5 oz

Calories 233 | Fat 7g | Carbohydrates 28g | Protein 17g

Preparation Time: 10 minutes | Cooking Time: 10 minutes

# Warm Barley, Chickpea, and Tomato Salad with Grilled Chicken

- 1 cup uncooked barley
- 12 oz chicken fillet
- 2 Tbs extra virgin olive oil
- 1 cup cherry tomatoes, halved
- 2 cups pre-cooked chickpeas
- Bunch of fresh sage
- 3 Tbs balsamic vinegar
- Salt
- Pepper

- Cook the barley in a large pot of salted water. Bring to a boil, then reduce heat to simmer over low for 30 minutes, or until tender. Drain, rinse and set aside for later.
- Meanwhile, grill the chicken for 2-3 minutes per side, or until cooked through.
- Once cool, slice the chicken and then set aside.
- Sauté the tomatoes in olive oil over medium heat for 1 minutes.
- Add the chickpeas, barley and sage. Toss and then let sit for 5 minutes.
- Add the chicken and heat through.
- Season to taste with the vinegar, salt and pepper and let sit for 1 minute before serving warm.

Servings: 8 | Serving Size: 3/4 cup

Calories 402 | Fat 0g | Carbohydrates 51g | Protein 21g

Preparation Time: 15 minutes | Cooking Time: 30 minutes

# Baked Lemon Chicken

- 4 boneless skinless chicken breasts
- 1 1/2 Tbs butter
- ⅓ cup chicken broth
- 4 Tbs fresh lemon juice
- 2 tsp minced garlic
- 1 tsp Italian seasoning
- salt and pepper to taste
- optional: fresh rosemary and lemon slices for garnish

- Preheat the oven to 400 degrees F.
- Melt the butter in a large, oven-safe skillet over medium high heat.
- Cook the chicken for 2-3 minutes, or until browned on each side.
- Meanwhile, whisk together the broth, lemon juice, garlic, seasoning, salt and pepper.
- Pour the sauce over the chicken and then bake for 20-30 minutes, or until the chicken is cooked through. Baste the chicken with the sauce at least once during the cooking.
- Garnish with rosemary and lemon before serving hot.

Servings: 4 | Yield: 5.9 oz | Calories 189 | Fat 8g | Carbohydrates 2g | Protein 0g
Preparation Time: 5 minutes | Cooking Time: 25 minutes

# Chicken and Asparagus Stir Fry

- 1 lb boneless skinless chicken breast, cut into bite size pieces
- 1 lb asparagus, trimmed
- 1 Tbs toasted sesame oil
- 1 tsp red pepper flakes
- 1/4 cup reduced sodium soy sauce
- 5 garlic cloves, minced
- 3 green onions, diced
- 1/2 Tbs sesame seeds
- Juice from 1 lime

- Combine the soy sauce, garlic, half of the oil and lime juice.
- Marinate the chicken in the mixture for at least 3 hours, or overnight.
- Sauté the red pepper flakes and asparagus in the remaining oil over medium high heat for 5-7 minutes, or until the asparagus is tender. Season to taste with salt and pepper.
- Remove from the pan and fry the chicken until cooked through, about 5 minutes per side.
- Return the asparagus to the pan and toss to heat.
- Garnish with green onions and sesame seeds before serving.

Servings: 4 | Yield: 6.4 oz | Calories 207 | Fat 5g | Carbohydrates 11g | Protein 3g
Preparation Time: 5 minutes | Cooking Time: 15 minutes | Inactive Time: 3 hours

# Bruschetta Stuffed Chicken Breasts

- 4 boneless skinless chicken breast halves
- 1 Tbs olive oil
- 4.5 oz mushrooms, chopped (canned or fresh)
- 5 cloves garlic, minced
- 1/4 tsp salt
- 1/2 cup red onion, chopped
- 1/2 cup fresh basil, chopped
- 3 roma tomatoes, chopped
- 4 tsp balsamic vinegar
- 1/8 tsp black pepper
- 1/4 cup parmesan cheese, shredded, optional
- 1/4 cup balsamic vinegar
- 1/3 cup fat free chicken broth
- 3 cloves garlic, minced
- 1 tsp Italian seasoning

- Preheat the oven to 350 degrees F and lightly grease a baking dish.
- Slice the chicken breasts so that a pocket is created along the long side of the breast. Be careful not to cut all the way through.
- Sauté the mushrooms and garlic in the olive oil for 1-2 minutes. Season with salt.
- Add the onion, basil, tomatoes, 4 tsp vinegar and pepper. Mix well and season to taste with additional salt. Cook for an additional 1-2 minutes, or until the onions become tender.
- Stuff the chicken with the bruschetta mixture.
- Bake for 20-30 minutes.
- Meanwhile, combine the vinegar, broth, garlic and Italian seasoning.
- Serve the chicken hot with the sauce, remaining bruschetta and parmesan cheese.

Servings: 4 | Yield: 11.9 oz | Calories 284 | Fat 9g | Carbohydrates 18g | Protein 5g
Preparation Time: 15 minutes | Cooking Time: 35 minutes

# Buffalo Chicken Wrap

- 2 Tbs hot sauce, or to taste
- 8 oz cooked chicken, diced
- ½ cup romaine
- ¼ cup diced tomatoes
- ¼ cup shredded Cheddar cheese
- 2 Tbs mayonnaise
- 2 tsp white vinegar
- 1 tsp fresh dill

- Combine the hot sauce and chicken.
- Combine the mayonnaise, vinegar and dill and mix well.
- Evenly divide the chicken between the two lettuce leaves and top with the tomatoes and cheese.
- Drizzle on the dill mayonnaise and serve.

Servings: 2 | Yield: 7.3 oz (half recipe) | Calories 129 | Fat 9g | Carbohydrates 6g | Protein 1g

Preparation Time: 10 minutes

# Chicken & Mushroom Risotto

- 1 cup uncooked short grain, white rice
- 2 1/2 cup chicken broth
- 4 chicken breasts, boneless, skinless
- 1 medium white onion, finely chopped
- 1 Tbs olive oil
- 2 cloves garlic, minced
- 2 (8 oz) cans mushrooms, drained and finely chopped
- 1/2 cup grated Parmesan cheese

- Combine the rice and 1 ½ cups of chicken broth in a saucepan and bring to a boil. Reduce heat to medium low and cook, covered, until the broth has absorbed.
- Meanwhile, fry the chicken breasts in a skillet until no longer pink, about 4-5 minutes per side. Remove from the pan and set aside.
- Add the onions, garlic and mushrooms with the olive oil. Cook for 3-4 minutes.
- Stir the cooked rice into the skillet and add the remaining broth.
- Cook, stirring frequently, until the liquid is absorbed.

Servings: 4 | Yield: 12.1 oz | Calories 444 | Fat 11g | Carbohydrates 46g | Protein 2g
Preparation Time: 5 minutes | Cooking Time: 25 minutes

# Chicken and Grape Salad

- 1 lb chicken breasts, cooked, cooled and diced into bite-sized pieces
- 2 cups seedless red grapes, halved
- ½ cup walnuts, chopped
- 1 medium celery stalk, chopped
- ½ cup mayo
- 1 tsp dry mustard
- 1 Tbs apple cider vinegar
- 2 Tbs chives, minced + extra for garnish

- Whisk together the mayonnaise, mustard, vinegar and chives.
- Mix together the chicken, grapes, walnuts and celery.
- Drizzle on the dressing and mix well. Serve chilled.

Servings: 8 | Yield: 4.4 oz | Calories 210 | Fat 11g | Carbohydrates 9g | Protein 1g

Preparation Time: 15 minutes

# Chicken and Peach Salad

- 1/2 cup carrots, grated
- 3 cups arugula
- 3/4 cup peach slices
- 1 cup chicken, sliced
- 1 tsp cinnamon
- 2 Tbsp coconut oil
- 1 tsp nutmeg

- Combine all ingredients in a bowl and drizzle on dressing of choice before serving.

Servings: 2 | Yield: 9.1 oz | Calories 193 | Fat 15g | Carbohydrates 12g | Protein 3g
Preparation Time: 10 minutes | Cooking Time: 3 minutes

# Chicken Bruschetta

- 1 Tbs olive oil
- 4 boneless, skinless chicken breasts
- 2 cups cherry or grape tomatoes, sliced
- 1 large onion, chopped
- 3 cloves garlic, minced
- 1 cup fresh basil leaves, packed
- 4 Tbs balsamic vinegar

- Fry the chicken in half of the olive oil for 5-6 minutes per side, or until cooked through.
- Meanwhile, prepare the vegetables.
- Remove the chicken from the pan and then sauté the onions and garlic in the oil for 2-3 minutes, or until tender.
- Add the tomatoes and basil, cooking for an additional 4-5 minutes.
- Stir in the vinegar and then return the chicken to the pan.
- Cook until the chicken is hot and serve immediately, garnished with additional fresh basil, if desired

Servings: 4 | Yield: 8.5 oz | Calories 255 | Fat 4g | Carbohydrates 17g | Protein 8g
Preparation Time: 10 minutes | Cooking Time: 20 minutes

# Chicken Cacciatore

- 1 lb Boneless Chicken Breast – Cubed
- 2 cans tomato paste (6 oz)
- 4 cloves garlic minced
- 1 Tbs dried parsley
- 1 Tbs dried basil
- salt & pepper to taste
- 2 cups chicken broth

- Combine all ingredients in a slow cooker and cook on low for 8 hours.
- Serve hot, topped with Parmesan cheese, if desired.

Servings: 4 | Yield: 11.4 oz | Calories 283 | Fat 5g | Carbohydrates 18g | Protein 4g
Preparation Time: 5 minutes | Cooking Time: 8 hours

# Chicken Salad Cabbage Wraps

- 3 cup cooked chicken
- 1 cup diced peeled mango
- 2 green onions - stems cut off
- 2 tsp white miso paste
- 1/2 tsp minced garlic (1 clove)
- 1/4 cup coconut milk
- 1/4 tsp Salt/pepper or to taste
- 2 Tbs fresh cilantro, chopped
- 2 tsp sesame oil
- 1 Tbs lime juice
- 1 cup cherry tomatoes, sliced
- 8 napa cabbage leaves

- Combine all ingredients except the cabbage leaves and mix well.
- Soften the cabbage leaves in the microwave for 30 seconds.
- Fill the cabbage leaves with about 1/3 cup of the chicken mixture each.
- Roll up the leaves and serve.

Servings: 8 | Yield: 6.3 oz | Calories 66 | Fat 4g | Carbohydrates 6g | Protein 1g

Preparation Time: 15 minutes

# Chipotle Lime Chicken Fajita Skewers

- 2 lbs chicken breast
- 5 limes (juiced)
- 1/2 Tbs sea salt
- 1/2 Tbs cumin
- 1 Tbs ground chipotle pepper
- 1/4 cup cilantro (chopped)
- 1 garlic clove (minced)
- 2 red bell peppers
- 2 green bell peppers
- 1 red onion

- Combine the juice of 4 limes, salt, cumin, chipotle, cilantro and garlic.
- Add the chicken and marinate for at least 30 minutes.
- Skewer the chicken and vegetables and grill for 5-7 minutes per side, or until the chicken is cooked through.
- Drizzle on the remaining lime juice and serve.

Servings: 6 | Yield: 11.6 oz | Calories 233 | Fat 4g | Carbohydrates 13g | Protein 4g
Preparation Time: 5 minutes | Cooking Time: 10 minutes | Inactive Time: 30 minutes

# Coconut Garlic Chicken

- 1 lb skinless, boneless chicken breasts, diced
- 1 Tbs coconut oil
- 1 14-15oz can light coconut milk
- 6 cloves garlic, minced
- 1/4 cup apple cider vinegar
- 1/4 cup fresh cilantro
- Salt and pepper to taste

- Fry the chicken in the coconut oil for 2-3 minutes per side on medium high heat.
- Add the vinegar and garlic and cook for 4-5 minutes, or until the vinegar is nearly gone.
- Stir in the coconut milk and reduce heat to medium. Cook for 8-10 minutes, or until slightly thickened.
- Season to taste with salt and pepper, then garnish with fresh cilantro before serving.

Servings: 4 | Yield: 4.9 oz | Calories 137 | Fat 10g | Carbohydrates 5g | Protein 0g
Preparation Time: 5 minutes | Cooking Time: 20 minutes

# Garlicky Chicken Thighs in Red Pepper Sauce

- 2 Tbs olive oil
- 8 bone-in skin-on chicken thighs (about 3 lbs.), trimmed of excess fat and skin
- Kosher salt and freshly ground black pepper
- 6 cloves garlic, smashed
- 2 tsp fresh thyme leaves
- 1 cup lower-salt chicken broth
- 3 jarred roasted red peppers, drained and cut into 1-inch strips (1-1/2 cups)
- 1 medium russet potato, peeled and cut into 3/4-inch dice (1-1/2 cups)
- 1 Tbs sherry vinegar

- Preheat the oven to 425 degrees F.
- Season the chicken with salt and pepper on both sides.
- Brown the chicken in a large, oven safe pan over medium high heat for about 3 minutes per side.
- Remove the chicken from the pan and add the garlic, cooking for 2-3 minutes.
- Add the broth, peppers, potato and vinegar and bring to a boil.
- Remove from heat and add the chicken.
- Bake for 30 minutes, or until the chicken is cooked through.

Servings: 6 | Yield: 8.3 oz | Calories 224 | Fat 9g | Carbohydrates 15g | Protein 2g
Preparation Time: 15 minutes | Cooking Time: 30 minutes

# Ground Turkey Patties with Tahini Yogurt Sauce

- 1 lb ground turkey breast
- 1 medium onion, finely diced
- 5 cloves garlic, minced
- 1/2 cup plain, nonfat Greek yogurt
- 3 Tbs tahini paste
- 1 Tbs olive oil

- 1 tsp onion powder
- 1 Tbs dried parsley
- Juice from 1 lemon
- Salt and pepper to taste

- Combine the yogurt, tahini, 1 clove garlic, lemon juice and salt and mix well. Refrigerate until serving.
- Combine the remaining ingredients and form into 16 small patties.
- Cook the patties for 3 minutes per side in a large skillet over high heat.
- Serve topped with the tahini sauce.

Servings: 4 | Yield: 7.2 oz | Calories 250 | Fat 11g | Carbohydrates 14g | Protein 2g
Preparation Time: 15 minutes | Cooking Time: 10 minutes

## Herbed Chicken & Potatoes

- 4 boneless skinless chicken breasts or 4-6 chicken thighs
- 3 cups chopped potatoes (about 1 ½ inch pieces)
- 3 Tbs oil
- 1 Tbs Italian seasoning blend
- 1 tsp garlic powder
- salt and pepper to taste,
- fresh herbs for garnish (optional)

- Combine the chicken and potatoes in a large bowl and season with the olive oil, salt, pepper, garlic powder and Italian seasoning. Mix well.
- Cook in a slow cooker for 4-6 hours on low before garnishing with herbs (oregano and basil) and serving.

Servings: 4 | Yield: 12.4 oz | Calories 354 | Fat 10g | Carbohydrates 60g | Protein 7g
Preparation Time: 5 minutes | Cooking Time: 6 minutes

# Lemon & Sesame Chicken

- 4 boneless skinless chicken breasts
- 1 egg white
- 2 Tbs sesame seeds
- 2 Tbs vegetable oil
- 1 onion, sliced
- 1 lemon, zested and juiced
- 3 Tbs chicken broth
- 7 oz water chestnuts, sliced

- Slice the chicken into strips about 1/2-inch thick.
- Beat the egg whites until foamy and then dip the chicken in the egg whites.
- Dip the chicken in sesame seeds.
- Heat the oil over medium heat in a large skillet and then stir fry the onion for 2 minutes.
- Add the chicken and cook for 5 minutes.
- Meanwhile, mix together the lemon zest, juice and broth.
- Pour the mixture into the pan and bring to a boil.
- Reduce heat and then stir in the chestnuts.
- Cook for 2 minutes.
- Sere hot, garnished with additional lemon peel.

Servings: 4 | Yield: 6.9 oz | Calories 266 | Fat 12g | Carbohydrates 9g | Protein 2g
Preparation Time: 10 minutes | Cooking Time: 10 minutes

# Mediterranean Chicken Salad with Fennel, Raisins & Pine Nuts

**For the dressing:**
- 1/2 small clove garlic, mashed to a paste with a pinch of kosher salt
- 3 Tbs mayonnaise
- 1 Tbs olive oil
- 1 Tbs fresh lemon juice, more as needed
- pinch cayenne

**For the salad:**
- 1 cup chopped or shredded chicken
- 1/3 cup small-diced fresh fennel
- 3 Tbs chopped sweet onion, such as Vidalia
- 2 Tbs toasted pine nuts
- 2 Tbs golden raisins
- 2 Tbs chopped fresh flat-leaf parsley
- Kosher salt and freshly ground pepper, to taste

- Combine the garlic, mayonnaise, oil, 1 Tbs lemon juice and cayenne pepper. Mix well and set aside.
- Combine the remaining ingredients in a large bowl and mix well.
- Drizzle on the dressing and refrigerate for 1 hour before serving.

Servings: 4 | Yield: 4.5 oz | Calories 148 | Fat 10g | Carbohydrates 13g | Protein 4g
Preparation Time: 10 minutes | Inactive Time: 1 hour

# Mushroom Parmesan Chicken

- 1 lb skinless, boneless chicken breasts, sliced into strips
- 1 lb portobello mushrooms, sliced
- 1 cup Parmesan cheese, grated
- 1 Tbs light butter
- 1/4 cup fat free chicken broth
- 5 garlic cloves, minced
- 1 tsp dried oregano
- 1 tsp dried basil
- 1 1/2 cups white wine
- 1 cup reduced fat milk
- Salt and pepper to taste

- Season the chicken with salt and pepper and fry in the butter until golden brown, about 3-5 minutes per side.
- Remove and set aside.
- Sauté the garlic and mushrooms for 5 minutes, adding more butter if needed.
- Return the chicken to the pan and add the wine, oregano and basil.
- Simmer for 15 minutes, or until the liquid is mostly gone.
- Stir in the milk and parmesan until the cheese is melted, about 3-5 minutes.
- Season to taste with salt and pepper before serving.

Servings: 6 | Yield: 11.3 oz | Calories 388 | Fat 9g | Carbohydrates 35g | Protein 5g
Preparation Time: 10 minutes | Cooking Time: 20 minutes

# Pan-Seared Tuna Steaks with Warm Tomato, Basil, and Olive Salad

- 4 5-oz. boneless, skinless tuna steaks
- Kosher salt and freshly ground black pepper
- 2 Tbs extra-virgin olive oil
- 1 medium shallot, finely chopped
- 2 cups mixed yellow and red grape or cherry tomatoes, halved
- 1/3 cup sliced pitted green olives, such as picholine or Cerignola
- 2 Tbs finely chopped fresh basil
- 1/2 Tbs fresh lemon juice

- Season the tuna with salt and pepper.
- Cook in a large skillet in the oil for 3-4 minutes per side, or until desired doneness.
- Remove from pan and sauté the shallot for 1 minute.
- Add the tomatoes, olives, basil, salt and pepper and cook for 2 minutes.
- Stir in the lemon juice and serve with the tuna.

Servings: 4 | Yield: 12.3 oz | Calories 371 | Fat 15g | Carbohydrates 22g | Protein 5g
Preparation Time: 5 minutes | Cooking Time: 10 minutes

# Pot-Roasted Mediterranean Chicken

- 3-1/2 lb whole chicken, rinsed and dried
- Sea salt and freshly ground black pepper to taste
- 2 sprigs fresh marjoram, 10 inches each, leaves stripped
- 7 sprigs fresh thyme, 4 inches each, leaves stripped
- 6 medium cloves garlic
- 5 Tbs olive oil
- 1 preserved lemon (or 1 fresh lemon), sliced 1/8-inch thick
- 7 oz pitted black olives, such as kalamata
- 9 oz button mushrooms
- 1/2 cup (1-1/2 oz.) sun-dried tomatoes, softened in very hot water
- 1 medium onion, cut into eighths

- Preheat the oven to 425 degrees F.
- Season the chicken with salt and pepper.
- Combine the marjoram, thyme, garlic and 1 Tbs olive oil and season the chicken with the paste.
- Place half of the olives and lemon slices along with a third of the mushrooms in the cavity.
- Place, breast side down, in a heavy pan and place the tomatoes around the chicken.
- Top with remaining vegetables and add oil.
- Bake for 2-3 hours, or until cooked through.
- Serve hot, garnished with the vegetables.

Servings: 4 | Yield: 8.7 oz | Calories 412 | Fat 32g | Carbohydrates 16g | Protein 3g
Preparation Time: 10 minutes | Cooking Time: 3 hours

# Roasted Red Pepper Chicken

- 1 lbs chicken breasts
- 1 Tbs light butter
- 1/4 cup onion, chopped
- 2 cloves garlic, minced
- 15 oz jar roasted red peppers, canned in water, drained and chopped
- 1 1/4 cup chicken broth
- 4 oz fat free cream cheese
- 1/2 tsp crushed red pepper, or to taste
- 1/4 cup chopped basil leaves

- Sear the chicken for 5 minutes in the butter and then remove and set aside.
- Sauté the garlic and onions over medium high heat for 2-3 minutes.
- Add the peppers and cook for an additional 2 minutes.
- Add the broth, cream cheese and crushed red pepper. Simmer for 10-15 minutes, or until the cheese is melted and sauce thickened.
- Add the basil and cook for 2 minutes.
- Return the chicken to the sauce and heat through.
- Season to taste with salt and pepper before serving.

Servings: 4 | Yield: 6.6 oz | Calories 110 | Fat 3g | Carbohydrates 9g | Protein 3g
Preparation Time: 5 minutes | Cooking Time: 20 minutes

# Spicy Pecan Crusted Chicken

- 2 lbs skinless, boneless chicken breasts cuts into 6 fillets
- 1/2 cup chopped pecans
- 2 tsp ground chipotle pepper
- 1 Tbs orange zest
- 2 large egg whites
- Salt and pepper to taste

- Pulse the pecans, zest, chipotle, salt and pepper in a food processor until the mixture resembles bread crumbs.
- Dip the chicken in the egg mixture, then in the pecan mixture.
- Fry in oil over medium high heat until cooked through, about 4-5 minutes per side.

Servings: 6 | Yield: 6.1 oz | Calories 319 | Fat 12g | Carbohydrates 2g | Protein 1g
Preparation Time: 15 minutes | Cooking Time: 15 minutes

# Tahini Chicken Salad

- 1 lb cooked chicken breast, chopped
- 2 cups kale, finely chopped
- 1 cups red cabbage, shredded
- 2 cups broccoli slaw
- 1 1/2 cups cherry tomatoes
- 1 medium red onion, thinly sliced
- 1/2 cup prepared tahini sauce
- Juice from 1 small lemon

- Combine all ingredients in a large bowl and mix well.
- Serve immediately or refrigerate until serving.

Servings: 4 | Yield: 8.4 oz | Calories 249 | Fat 10g | Carbohydrates 14g | Protein 6g

Preparation Time: 5 minutes


# Turkey Chow Mein with Zucchini

- 3 zucchini (small-medium)
- 1/2 lb leftover roasted turkey or uncooked turkey breast (diced or sliced into strips)
- 1 cup bean sprouts
- 1 small red chili pepper, chopped
- 1 tsp sesame oil
- 2-3 tbsp avocado oil or peanut oil
- 1/4 tsp white pepper
- Sea salt
- 1 bunch scallions, cut 1-2 inches
- 1 garlic clove, minced
- Sesame seeds
- **Sauce**
- 1/4 tsp baking soda
- 1 Tbs rice wine vinegar
- 2 Tbs soy sauce
- 2 tsp chili paste (or Sriracha)
- 2-3 garlic cloves, minced
- 2 tsp grated ginger or 1/2 tsp ground ginger

- Combine the sauce ingredients and add half of it to the turkey.
- Sauté the garlic in oil for 1 minute.
- Add the turkey and sprouts and cook until meat is cooked through.
- Add the zucchini noodles and sauce and cook for 2-3 minutes, stirring frequently.
- Add the scallions and pepper and mix well before garnishing with sesame seeds and chili flakes and serving.

Servings: 3 | Yield: 13.1 oz | Calories 231 | Fat 13g | Carbohydrates 16g | Protein 3g
Preparation Time: 10 minutes | Cooking Time: 15 minutes

# Turkey Taco Soup

- 1 lb ground turkey
- 1/2 cup fat free chicken broth
- 2 28oz cans diced, roasted tomatoes
- 1 15 oz can black beans (drained & rinsed)
- 1 15oz can pinto beans (drained & rinsed)
- 1 cup corn
- 1 medium onion, diced
- 3 cloves garlic, minced
- 1 packet taco seasoning mix
- 1 packet ranch seasoning mix
- 1/2 cup reduced fat sharp cheddar, shredded

- Cook the turkey until no longer pink.
- Add the garlic and onion and cook for an additional 2-3 minutes.
- Add the seasonings, tomatoes, corn, beans and broth and bring to a simmer. Cook, covered, for 20-30 minutes.
- Serve, topped with cheese, sour cream, limes, onions and cilantro.

Servings: 6 | Yield: 19.5 oz | Calories 349 | Fat 4g | Carbohydrates 35g | Protein 9g
Preparation Time: 10 minutes | Cooking Time: 30 minutes

# Tuscan Chicken

- 1 lb skinless, boneless chicken breasts, thinly sliced
- 10 oz fresh baby spinach leaves
- 1 large red bell pepper, julienne cut
- 4 cloves garlic, minced
- 2 tsp dried oregano
- 2 tsp dried basil
- 2 Tbs butter
- 1 cup grated Parmesan cheese
- 1 cup fat free milk
- 1/2 cup fat free chicken broth
- Salt and pepper to taste

- Season the chicken with the oregano, basil, salt and pepper.
- Fry in the butter until golden brown and cooked through, about 3-4 minutes per side.
- Add the peppers and garlic with 2 Tbs broth to the pan and cook for 1-2 minutes.
- Add in the spinach and milk and cook until the spinach is wilted, about 2 minutes.
- Stir in the parmesan cheese until melted and combined, about 3-4 minutes.
- Serve hot.

Servings: 6 | Yield: 8.2 oz | Calories 148 | Fat 8g | Carbohydrates 9g | Protein 2g
Preparation Time: 5 minutes | Cooking Time: 15 minutes

# Vegetable Chicken Soup

- 1 Tbs oil
- 1 medium onion, chopped
- 2 cloves garlic, minced
- 2 cups carrots, chopped
- 2 cups turnips, chopped
- 1 lb cooked and chopped chicken
- 8 cups chicken broth
- 2 cups frozen peas
- 1/2 tsp ground thyme
- Salt & pepper to taste

- Sauté the onion and garlic in the oil for 2 minutes.
- Add the carrots, turnips, chicken and broth. Simmer for 10-15 minutes, or until the vegetables are tender.
- Add the peas and thyme and season to taste with salt and pepper.
- Cook for 4-6 minutes, or until peas are done. Season to taste and serve.

Servings: 6 | Yield: 17 oz | Calories 159 | Fat 5g | Carbohydrates 16g | Protein 4g
Preparation Time: 5 minutes | Cooking Time: 20 minutes

# Winter Chicken Salad

- 1 lb skinless, boneless chicken breasts, cooked and sliced into strips
- 5 cups Romaine lettuce, chopped
- 2 cups red cabbage, shredded
- 1 small red onion, thinly sliced
- 1 pear, cored and diced
- 2 persimmons, peeled, seeded, and diced
- 1/2 cup pomegranate
- 1/3 cup pine nuts, toasted
- 2 Tbs walnut oil (you can use olive oil if preferred)
- 1/3 cup red wine vinegar
- Salt and pepper to taste

- Combine all ingredients and mix well.
- Season to taste and serve.

Servings: 6 | Yield: 7.8 oz | Calories 238 | Fat 10g | Carbohydrates 15g | Protein 4g

Preparation Time: 15 minutes

# Salads

# Asian Quinoa Salad

- For the Salad:
- 1 cup quinoa
- 2 cups chicken broth
- 1/4 tsp salt
- 1 cup chopped red cabbage
- 1 cup shelled and cooked edamame
- 1 red bell pepper, chopped
- 1/2 cup shredded carrots
- 1 cup diced cucumber

- For the dressing:
- 1/4 cup low sodium soy sauce
- 1 Tbs sesame oil
- 1 Tbs rice vinegar
- 2 Tbs chopped green onion
- 1/4 cup chopped cilantro
- 1 Tbs sesame seeds
- 1/4 tsp grated ginger
- 1/8 tsp red pepper flakes
- Salt and black pepper, to taste

- Bring the chicken stock, quinoa and salt to a boil over medium heat.
- Reduce heat to a simmer and cook for 15-20 minutes, or until the liquid is absorbed.
- Combine the quinoa, cabbage, edamame, pepper, carrots and cucumber.
- Whisk together the dressing ingredients and mix well.
- Pour the dressing over the quinoa and mix well before serving.

Servings: 4 | Serving Size: 19.2 oz

Calories 352 | Fat 10g | Carbohydrates 51g | Protein 18g

Preparation Time: 10 minutes | Cooking Time: 20 minutes

# Avocado Potato Salad

- 12 oz mini red potatoes
- 1.5-2 tbsp olive oil
- 1 tsp lemon zest
- 2 Tbs fresh lemon juice
- 3 Tbs fresh dill, minced
- 1 clove garlic, minced
- About 10 cherry tomatoes, halved or quartered
- 1 ripe avocado
- Salt and pepper

- Boil the potatoes in water for 15-20 minutes, or until tender.
- Remove from heat and immediately cool in cold water.
- Cut in quarters and combine with the remaining ingredients, except the avocado.
- Season to taste with salt and pepper.
- Top with the avocado and then serve immediately.

Servings: 4 | Serving Size: 16.6 oz

Calories 438 | Fat 14g | Carbohydrates 73g | Protein 9g

Preparation Time: 15 minutes | Cooking Time: 20 minutes

*Note: The potatoes can also be cooked in a microwave until tender instead of boiling.

# Avocado Salmon Salad with Kale

- 3/4 lb skinless, boneless salmon fillet
- 1 avocado, pitted, peeled and chopped, divided
- 2 Tbs lemon juice
- 6 cups baby kale
- 2 Tbs chopped pickled jalapeño peppers, or to taste

- Preheat the oven to 400 degrees F and line a baking pan with parchment paper.
- Place the salmon, skin side down, on the prepared sheet and bake for 10-12 minutes, or until cooked through.
- Flake the salmon with a fork and set asdie.
- Meanwhile, combine the avocado, lemon juice and 1 Tbs of water in a bowl and mix well.
- Stir in the kale.
- Evenly divide the kale between 4 plates and top with the salmon.
- Top the salmon with the remaining avocado and jalapenos before serving.

Servings: 4 | Serving Size: 8.4 oz

Calories 223 | Fat 11g | Carbohydrates 13g | Protein 21g

Preparation Time: 5 minutes | Cooking Time: 12 minutes

# Kale, Carrot and Avocado Salad

- 1 bunch kale, stemmed and finely chopped
- 2 cups grated carrots
- 1/2 avocado, peeled and pitted
- 1/4 cup thinly sliced red onion
- 2 Tbs lemon or lime juice
- 2 Tbs sesame seeds, toasted
- 1/2 tsp reduced sodium soy sauce

- Combine all ingredients, except the avocado, and mix well.
- Allow the salad to sit for 30 minutes at room temperature before serving to allow the kale to soften.
- Stir in the avocado immediately before serving.

Servings: 4 | Serving Size: 4.1 oz

Calories 97 | Fat 6g | Carbohydrates 11g | Protein 2g

Preparation Time: 5 minutes | Inactive Time: 30 minutes

# Bacalao (Salted Cod Salad)

- 1 lb salted cod
- 1 large yellow onion, thinly sliced
- 1 large tomato, diced
- ½ large avocado or a whole small avocado, diced
- 3 hard-boiled eggs, quartered
- 12 green olives (optional)
- ¼ cup olive oil
- 1 Tbs chicken or vegetable stock

- Soak the cod in cold water for 15-30 minutes. Drain and place in a large pot.
- Cover the cod with water and bring to a boil.
- Change the water and bring to a simmer another 3-4 times, or until the cod is reduced to the appropriate saltiness.
- Drain and break the cod into pieces.
- Sauté the onion with olive oil for 5-6 minutes, or until soft.
- Combine all ingredients in a bowl and mix well.
- Serve with rice and drizzled with olive oil.

Servings: 4 | Serving Size: 12.1 oz

Calories 613 | Fat 28g | Carbohydrates 9g | Protein 78g

Preparation Time: 30 minutes | Inactive Time: 30 minutes

# Barley and Bean Salad with Herb Pesto

- Herb Pesto:
- 1/2 cup lightly packed basil leaves
- 1/2 cup lightly packed parsley leaves
- 1/2 cup finely chopped kale (about 1 large leaf)
- 3 cloves roasted garlic (about 2 teaspoons)
- 1/2 cup walnut halves
- 3 Tbs chicken stock
- 1/4 tsp fine sea salt
- 1/2 tsp freshly ground black pepper

- Salad:
- 3/4 cup pearl barley
- 1 (15-ounce) can no-salt added pinto beans, drained
- 2 heirloom tomatoes, diced
- 1 avocado, peeled and diced
- 2/3 cup corn

- Combine the pesto ingredients in a food processor with 1 Tbs of water. Puree and then refrigerate until using.
- Combine the barley with 2 cups of water and bring to a boil.
- Lower heat and cover. Simmer for 35 minutes, or until most of the water has be absorbed and the barley is tender.
- Remove the barley from the heat and let sit for 5 minutes, covered.
- Layer barley, beans, tomatoes, avocado and corn in a bowl.
- Top with the pesto and then toss before serving.

Servings: 6 | Serving Size: 7.9 oz

Calories 304 | Fat 12g | Carbohydrates 44g | Protein 11g

Preparation Time: 10 minutes | Cooking Time: 35 minutes

# Chickpea, Avocado, & Feta Salad

- 1 can chickpeas, rinsed and drained
- 2 avocados, pitted, and chopped
- 1/3 cup chopped cilantro
- 2 Tbs green onion
- 1/3 cup feta cheese
- Juice of 1 lime
- Salt and black pepper, to taste

- Combine all ingredients in a bowl and season with salt and pepper.
- Serve immediately.

Servings: 4 | Serving Size: 7.7 oz

Calories 274 | Fat 18g | Carbohydrates 23g | Protein 9g

Preparation Time: 5 minutes | Cooking Time: 5 minutes

# Cobb Salad

- 6 cups chopped romaine heart lettuce
- 2 ripe avocados, seeded and peeled, slice into 1" pieces
- 1 split chicken breast, cooked, skin removed and cubed
- 2 vine-ripe tomatoes, chopped
- 2 hard-boiled eggs, peeled and sliced
- Dressing
- 1/4 cup red-chicken or vegetable stock vinegar
- 1/2 cup extra-virgin olive oil
- Kosher or sea salt to taste
- 1/8 tsp black pepper

- Combine all ingredients in a large bowl and then drizzle on the dressing.

Servings: 6 | Serving Size: 2-1/4 cups

Calories 282 | Fat 0g | Carbohydrates 8g | Protein 10g

Preparation Time: 15 minutes

# Grilled Corn & Zucchini Salad with Sun-Dried Tomato Vinaigrette

- Vegetables
- 6 ears corn, with husk
- 2 zucchini, sliced
- 1 Tbs olive oil
- Sea salt and black pepper
- Dressing
- 1/2 cup packed sun-dried tomatoes (soaked in hot water 10 minutes)
- 1 cup hot water
- 3 Tbs lemon juice
- 1 cup tightly packed fresh basil
- 4 cloves garlic, smashed
- 1/3 cup olive oil
- pinch each sea salt + black pepper, plus more to taste
- Fresh lime juice

- Brush the zucchini with the oil and season with salt and pepper.
- Soak the corn in cold water for 5 minutes.
- Meanwhile, combine all the dressing ingredients and blend on high in a blender or food processor. Add a little water to thin, if desired.
- Season to taste.
- Grill the corn for 5-8 minutes, rotating frequently, or until lightly browned.
- Remove from the husk and grill for another 5-8 minutes, turning frequently.
- When the corn is almost done, grill the zucchini for 2-4 minutes per side.
- Cut the corn off the cob and combine with the zucchini and chickpeas (if using).
- Drizzle on the lime juice and dressing and serve, garnished with basil.

Servings: 4 | Serving Size: 16.4 oz

Calories 429 | Fat 24g | Carbohydrates 55g | Protein 9g

Preparation Time: 10 minutes | Cooking Time: 20 minutes

# Jicama, Black Bean and Quinoa Salad

- 1 cup quinoa
- 2 Tbs rice vinegar
- Zest and juice of 2 limes
- Zest and juice of 1 orange
- 1 medium jicama (about 1 pound), peeled and diced
- 1 red bell pepper, seeded and diced
- 1/4 cup finely chopped fresh cilantro, plus more for garnish
- 2 cups cooked black beans, or 1 (15-ounce) can no-salt-added black beans, rinsed and drained
- 2 Tbs toasted sesame seeds

- Combine the quinoa and 2 cups of water in a saucepan and bring to a simmer. Cook, covered, for 15-20 minutes, or until the liquid is mostly absorbed and the quinoa is tender.
- Whisk together the vinegar, lime juice and zest and orange juice and zest.
- Combine the jicama, pepper, cilantro, beans and quinoa and mix well.
- Pour the dressing over the top and mix.
- Let sit for at least 10 minutes and then garnish with cilantro and sesame seeds before serving.

Servings: 6 | Serving Size: 12.3 oz

Calories 292 | Fat 4g | Carbohydrates 56g | Protein 11g

Preparation Time: 10 minutes | Cooking Time: 20 minutes

# Lemon Chicken Breasts with Asparagus & Salad

- Chicken
- 1 lb boneless, skinless chicken breasts
- 3 Tbs fresh squeezed lemon juice
- 3 Tbs olive oil plus 2 teaspoons, divided
- 4 Tbs chopped rosemary sprigs
- 4 Tbs chopped thyme
- 2 garlic cloves, minced
- 1/2 tsp crushed red pepper flakes
- 1/2 tsp kosher or sea salt
- Asparagus
- 1 lb asparagus, cleaned and woody bottoms removed (about 1-inch from bottom)
- 1 Tbs extra-virgin olive oil
- 1/4 tsp kosher or sea salt
- 1/4 tsp pepper
- Salad
- 4 cups mixed greens
- 1 cup halved tomatoes
- 3 Tbs vinaigrette

- Pound the chicken breasts to an even thickness, about ¾-inch thick.
- Whisk together the lemon juice, garlic, herbs, salt, pepper and 3 Tb of the olive oil.
- Marinate the chicken in the lemon juice mixture for at least 30 minutes, or up to 2 hours.
- Sear the chicken in hot olive oil over medium high heat for 1 minute per side.
- Reduce the heat to low and cook for 10 minutes, covered.
- Remove the pan from the heat and allow to sit for another 10 minutes, covered.
- Use a meat thermometer or slice open a breast to make sure they are not still pink in the middle.
- While the chicken cooks, preheat the oven to 400 degrees F.
- Combine the asparagus, olive oil, salt and pepper. Spread into an even layer on a sheet pan.
- Roast for 18-20 minutes, or until tender. Stir the asparagus halfway through the cooking time.
- Combine the green and tomatoes and drizzle on the dressing.
- Serve the chicken with the asparagus and the salad on the side.

Servings: 4 | Serving Size: 11 oz

Calories 229 | Fat 17g | Carbohydrates 21g | Protein 8g

Preparation Time: 10 minutes | Cooking Time: 25 minutes

*Note: If unable to find a vinaigrette without sugar, the following recipe works well.

¼ cup high quality balsamic vinegar, 1 Tbs minced garlic, ½ tsp salt, ½ tsp pepper, ¾ cup olive oil. Combine in a bowl or jar with lid and mix well.

# Mediterranean Salad

- 1 (15-ounce) can no-salt-added garbanzo beans, drained
- 1 cucumber, chopped
- 1 cup small broccoli florets
- 1 cup grape tomatoes, halved
- 1 cup finely sliced kale, tough stems removed
- 1/2 cup finely chopped red onion
- 2 Tbs finely chopped Kalamata olives
- 3 Tbs chicken or vegetable stock
- 1 clove garlic, minced
- 1 Tbs chopped fresh parsley
- 1 tsp chopped fresh thyme

- Combine all ingredients and mix well.
- Chill for 1 hour and then serve.

Servings: 4 | Serving Size: 10.4 oz

Calories 139 | Fat 3g | Carbohydrates 22g | Protein 8g

Preparation Time: 5 minutes | Inactive Time: 1 hour

# Mediterranean Tuna Salad

- 1 (6-ounce) can or jar of tuna, packed in water
- 1/2 cup artichoke hearts, diced
- 1/2 cup pitted kalamata olives, chopped
- 1 roasted red pepper, chopped
- 1/4 cup fresh chopped parsley
- 2 Tbs slivered basil leaves
- 3 Tbs olive oil
- Juice of 1 lemon
- Salt and fresh ground pepper, to taste

- Combine all ingredients and mix well. Serve with wrapped in lettuce leaves.

Servings: 2 | Serving Size: 1 cup

Calories 337 | Fat 0g | Carbohydrates 14g | Protein 20g

Preparation Time: 15 minutes

# Pan Fried Salmon with Asparagus & Warm Quinoa Salad

- 4 4 oz salmon fillets
- 1 Tbs extra-virgin olive oil
- 1 bunch asparagus, woody bottom stems removed
- 1 cup (dry) quinoa
- 1 ½ cups chicken or vegetable broth
- 1 red bell pepper, stemmed, seeded, and chopped
- 1 yellow or orange bell pepper, stemmed, seeded, and chopped
- 1/4 cup chopped parsley
- 2 Tbs freshly squeezed lemon juice, divided
- 1 tsp kosher or sea salt, divided
- 1/4 tsp black pepper

- Bring the quinoa and chicken or vegetable broth to a boil over medium high heat.
- Reduce heat to medium low and cook for 20-25 minutes, or until the broth is absorbed.
- Meanwhile, blanch the asparagus for 3-4 minutes in boiling water.
- Remove and immerse in ice water to stop cooking.
- Season the salmon with salt and pepper and cook the fillets in a little oil in the pan for 3-4 minutes per side, or until cooked to desired doneness.
- Add the pepper, parsley, 1 Tbs lemon juice and salt to taste to the quinoa.
- Top the quinoa with the asparagus and place the salmon on top before serving.
- Bring the quinoa and chicken or vegetable broth to a boil over medium high heat.
- Reduce heat to medium low and cook for 20-25 minutes, or until the broth is absorbed.
- Meanwhile, blanch the asparagus for 3-4 minutes in boiling water.
- Remove and immerse in ice water to stop cooking.
- Season the salmon with salt and pepper and cook the fillets in a little oil in the pan for 3-4 minutes per side, or until cooked to desired doneness.
- Add the pepper, parsley, 1 Tbs lemon juice and salt to taste to the quinoa.
- Top the quinoa with the asparagus and place the salmon on top before serving.

Servings: 4 | Serving Size: 1-3/4 cups quinoa salad, 3-4 spears asparagus and 1 salmon fillet

Calories 308 | Fat 0g | Carbohydrates 27g | Protein 20g

Preparation Time: 10 minutes | Cooking Time: 25 minutes

# Quinoa Kale Tomato Corn Salad

- 1 cup cooked quinoa
- 2 cups kale chopped
- 1 cup cherry tomatoes halved
- 1/2 cup corn
- 1 scallion chopped
- 1 garlic clove minced
- zest and juice from 1 lemon
- 2 Tbs extra virgin olive oil
- salt and freshly ground pepper to taste
- freshly grated Bellevitano cheese or your favorite cheese

- Combine all ingredients in a bowl and mix well. Serve immediately, or refrigerate until serving.

Servings: 2 | Serving Size: 11.9 oz

Calories 546 | Fat 21g | Carbohydrates 75g | Protein 18g

Preparation Time: 15 minutes | Cooking Time: 15 minutes

# Shrimp and Feta Salad Bowl

- 1 1/2 cups cleaned, deveined, and shelled raw shrimp
- 1/2 cup (low-fat) feta cheese, cubed or crumbled
- 1/4 cup roasted red peppers
- 1 cup halved cherry tomatoes
- 1/2 cup balsamic vinegar
- 1/2 cup coarsely chopped parsley
- 4 cups mixed salad greens
- 1/4 tsp kosher or sea salt
- 1/4 tsp black pepper
- 1/2 tsp extra-virgin olive oil

- Heat the balsamic in a small saucepan over medium heat for about 8 minutes, or until the vinegar becomes syrupy.
- Cook the shrimp in salted, boiling water for about 2 minutes, then drain and place in ice water to cool.
- Combine the greens, peppers, tomatoes, olive oil, salt and pepper. Mix well.
- Top with the feta and shrimp and drizzle on the vinegar.
- Garnish with fresh, chopped parsley before serving.

Servings: 2 | Serving Size: 15.5 oz

Calories 282 | Fat 11g | Carbohydrates 21g | Protein 23g

Preparation Time: 10 minutes | Cooking Time: 10 minutes

# Southwest Chickpea Salad

- 1 15 oz can black beans, rinsed & drained
- 1 15 oz can chickpeas, rinsed & drained
- 1 15 oz can corn
- 1 pint cherry tomatoes, chopped in half
- 2 medium avocado, diced
- 1 small can of diced olives
- Juice of one lime
- 2 Tbs extra virgin olive oil
- 1 tsp cumin
- ¼ tsp chili powder
- ¼ tsp salt
- 1/4 cup cilantro, chopped
- ¼ cup feta cheese for garnish (optional)

- Combine all ingredients and mix well.
- Serve immediately, or refrigerate until serving.

Servings: 6 | Serving Size: 9.3 oz

Calories 300 | Fat 16g | Carbohydrates 35g | Protein 9g

Preparation Time: 10 minutes

# Sriracha Lime Chicken Chopped Salad

- Sriracha Lime Chicken
- 2 organic chicken breasts
- 3 Tbs sriracha
- 1 lime, juiced
- 1/4 tsp fine sea salt
- 1/4 tsp freshly ground pepper
- Salad
- 4 cups lettuce, chopped
- 8 pineapple slices, using pineapple corer
- 1 cup organic grape tomatoes
- 1/3 cup red onion, finely chopped
- 1 avocado, cubed
- Lime Vinaigrette
- 1/3 cup light olive oil
- 1/4 cup apple cider vinegar
- 2 limes, juiced
- dash fine sea salt

- Season the chicken with salt and pepper on both sides.
- Spread on the sriracha and lime and let the chicken sit for 20 minutes.
- Cook the chicken for 3-4 minutes per side over medium heat, or until done.
- Grill the pineapple with the chicken.
- Meanwhile, whisk together the dressing and season to taste.
- Dress the salad and serve as a side to the chicken and pineapple.

Servings: 4 | Serving Size: 16.4 oz

Calories 484 | Fat 28g | Carbohydrates 32g | Protein 30g

Preparation Time: 10 minutes | Cooking Time: 15 minutes | Inactive Time: 20 minutes

# Taco Salad in a Jar

- Salad:
- 1/2 lb ground turkey
- 1 tsp chili powder
- 1/2 tsp cumin
- 1/4 tsp garlic powder
- 1/4 tsp sea salt
- 1/2 cup shredded cheddar cheese, reduced-fat
- 3 cups chopped romaine lettuce
- 1 cup halved cherry tomatoes
- 1/2 cup salsa
- Creamy Salsa Dressing: (optional)
- 2 Tbs plain Greek yogurt
- 2 Tbs ripe, mashed avocado
- Juice of 1 lime
- 1/4 cup salsa

- Brown the turkey in a skillet over medium high heat until cooked through.
- Add the spices and mix well. Allow the meat to cool before layering the salad.
- Place the salsa in the bottom of a jar or bow and top with the turkey, tomatoes, lettuce and cheese.
- Combine the dressing ingredients in a blender or bowl and mix well.
- Drizzle on the dressing before serving.

Servings: 6 | Serving Size: 1-1/4 cup

Calories 196 | Fat 0g | Carbohydrates 9g | Protein 15g

Preparation Time: 10 minutes | Cooking Time: 10 minutes

# Turkey Burgers with Cucumber Salad

- Turkey burgers
- 1 lb lean ground turkey
- 1 large egg, beaten
- 1/2 cup oatmeal
- 1/3 cup grated or finely chopped onions
- 1/3 cup finely chopped parsley
- 1 clove garlic, minced
- 1/2 tsp kosher or sea salt
- 1/2 tsp black pepper
- 1 Tbs extra-virgin olive oil
- 2 tsp canola oil or cooking spray to lightly coat the pan or grill
- Cucumber salad
- 1 cucumber, diced small
- 1/2 cup chopped chives or green onions
- 1 medium-sized ripe tomato, finely diced
- 2 Tbs freshly squeezed lime or lemon juice
- 1/4 tsp kosher or sea salt

- Combine the turkey burger ingredients, except oil, and mix well.
- Form into 4 patties.
- Lightly grease the grill and grill the patties for 5-6 minutes per side on medium high.
- Meanwhile, combine the cucumber salad ingredients and chill until serving.

Servings: 4 | Serving Size: 1 patty and 1/4 cup salad

Calories 314 | Fat 0g | Carbohydrates 15g | Protein 26g

Preparation Time: 15 minutes | Cooking Time: 15 minutes

# Watermelon, Tomato and Goat Cheese Salad

- 2 cups watermelon, diced
- 1 cup cherry tomatoes, cut in half
- 1 cup cucumber, peeled, diced
- 1 Tbs goat cheese, crumbled
- 2 Tbs mint leaves, sliced thin
- 1 Tbs balsamic dressing
- ¼ tsp salt
- ¼ tsp pepper

- Combine all the ingredients, except the goat cheese and mix well.
- Top with the goat cheese and serve immediately, or chill until serving.

Servings: 4 | Serving Size: 5.9 oz

Calories 55 | Fat 2g | Carbohydrates 11g | Protein 2g

Preparation Time: 15 minutes | Cooking Time: 15 minutes

*Note: If unable to find a balsamic dressing without sugar, the following recipe works well.

¼ cup high quality balsamic vinegar, 1 Tbs minced garlic, ½ tsp salt, ½ tsp pepper, ¾ cup olive oil. Combine in a bowl or jar with lid and mix well.

# Zucchini "Pasta" Salad with Pesto, Mozzarella and Tomatoes

- 2 medium zucchini, spiral sliced
- 12 big fresh basil leaves
- 2 Tbs grated Parmesan cheese
- 1 Tbs pine nuts
- 1 clove garlic
- 1/4 tsp salt
- 1/8 cup extra virgin olive oil
- 1 cup cherry tomatoes, halved or quartered
- 1/2 cup Mozzarella, drained from its water and chopped
- 1 avocado, diced

- Pulse the pine nuts, basil, garlic, salt and parmesan in a food processor until well combined.
- With the food processor running, drizzle in the olive oil until well combined.
- Toss all ingredients in a bowl and serve immediately.

Servings: 4 | Serving Size: 7.8 oz

Calories 226 | Fat 19g | Carbohydrates 10g | Protein 8g

Preparation Time: 15 minutes

*Note: If desired, sauté the zucchini noodles in 1 Tbs of olive oil for 3-4 minutes, or until tender, before mixing with the pesto.

# Side Dishes

# Baked Sweet Potatoes with Crispy Kale and Feta

- 4 large sweet potatoes
- 4 oz small bunch curly kale, center ribs removed and cut into bite size pieces
- 1 Tbs olive oil
- 1 tsp sea salt
- 1/2 tsp black pepper
- 1/2 cup walnut pieces
- 3/4 cup crumbled feta cheese

- Preheat the oven to 400 degrees F.
- Pierce the potatoes with a fork and then wrap in foil.
- Bake for 45-55 minutes, or until tender.
- Meanwhile, combine the kale, olive oil, salt and pepper in a skillet.
- Sauté over medium heat for 5 minutes, or until the kale is wilted.
- Slice the potatoes in half and remove some of the pulp to mix with the kale, feta and walnuts.
- Place the kale mixture back into the potato skin and bake for another 10 minutes to melt the feta before serving.

Servings: 8 | Serving Size: 1/2 sweet potato (about 3.6 oz)

Calories 164 | Fat 10g | Carbohydrates 16g | Protein 5g

Preparation Time: 10 minutes | Cooking Time: 1 hour

# Cauliflower Fried Rice

- 1 large onion, diced
- 1 1/2 cup carrots, diced
- 2 Tbs coconut oil
- 1 tsp salt
- 1 tsp ground ginger, or to taste
- 1 tsp garlic powder
- 1 large cauliflower, grated
- 1/2 cup coconut aminos
- 2 eggs, scrambled
- 1/2 cup diced green onions

- Sauté the onion and carrots in the coconut oil over medium heat for 7-9 minutes, or until tender.
- Season with salt, ginger and garlic.
- Add the cauliflower and coconut aminos and cook for 5 minutes, stirring continuously.
- Push the cauliflower and carrot mixture to the side and add the scrambled eggs.
- Cook, stirring constantly, until set and then stir in the vegetables.
- Garnish with green onion before serving.

Servings: 6 | Serving Size: 7 oz

Calories 131 | Fat 7g | Carbohydrates 12g | Protein 7g

Preparation Time: 10 minutes | Cooking Time: 17 minutes

# Cauliflower Tabbouleh with Green Olives

- 3 Tbs freshly squeezed lemon juice
- 3 Tbs extra virgin olive oil
- ½ tsp sea salt
- Freshly ground black pepper to taste
- 1 small head of cauliflower, cut into florets
- 3 medium stalks of celery, finely sliced
- 1-2 green spring onions, finely chopped
- ¼ cup green olives, coarsely chopped
- 1 large bunch or two small bunches of fresh flat-leaf parsley, finely chopped
- 1 large bunch fresh mint leaves, finely chopped
- ¼ cup walnuts, coarsely chopped

- Whisk together the lemon juice, olive oil, salt and pepper.
- Place the cauliflower in a food processor and process until it resembles rice.
- Combine the cauliflower, green onions, celery and olives to the dressing and mix well.
- Mix in the chopped herbs and season to taste with salt and pepper.

Serve, garnished with chopped walnuts.

Servings: 6 | Serving Size: 5.7 oz

Calories 134 | Fat 11g | Carbohydrates 8g | Protein 3g

Preparation Time: 15 minutes

# Grilled Pumpkin and Carrot over Quinoa

- 1 cup quinoa (any color- white, red, black, golden, or a mix)
- 2 cups chicken broth
- 1/4 cup raw almonds
- 2 medium carrots, peeled, cut in half crosswise and then cut lengthwise
- 1 (1 to 1-1/2 pound) butternut squash, peeled, seeded, and cut into halves
- 1/2 cup fresh basil leaves, divided
- 2 Tbs freshly squeezed lemon juice
- 3 Tbs olive oil, divided
- 1 tsp kosher or sea salt
- 1/4 tsp pepper

- Combine the quinoa and chicken broth in a saucepan and bring to a boil.
- Reduce heat and cook for 15 minutes, covered, or until all the liquid is absorbed.
- Uncover and cool for 15 minutes.
- Meanwhile, combine the squash, carrots, 1 Tbs olive oil, ¼ tsp salt and a ¼ tsp pepper and mix well.
- Grill on medium high for 5-7 minutes per side, or until tender. Set aside.
- Toast the almonds for about 3 minutes over medium high heat, stirring constantly, until toasted but not burned.
- Whisk together 2 Tbs lemon juice, 2 Tbs olive oil and 1/8 tsp salt and mix well. Stir in ¼ cup of basil.
- Combine the quinoa and dressing and mix well. Season to taste with remaining salt and pepper.
- Top with the squash and carrots and sprinkle on the remaining basil and almonds before serving.
- Combine the quinoa and chicken broth in a saucepan and bring to a boil.
- Reduce heat and cook for 15 minutes, covered, or until all the liquid is absorbed.
- Uncover and cool for 15 minutes.
- Meanwhile, combine the squash, carrots, 1 Tbs olive oil, ¼ tsp salt and a ¼ tsp pepper and mix well.
- Grill on medium high for 5-7 minutes per side, or until tender. Set aside.
- Toast the almonds for about 3 minutes over medium high heat, stirring constantly, until toasted but not burned.
- Whisk together 2 Tbs lemon juice, 2 Tbs olive oil and 1/8 tsp salt and mix well. Stir in ¼ cup of basil.

- Combine the quinoa and dressing and mix well. Season to taste with remaining salt and pepper.
- Top with the squash and carrots and sprinkle on the remaining basil and almonds before serving.

Servings: 6 | Serving Size: 9.6 oz

Calories 289 | Fat 12g | Carbohydrates 39g | Protein 10g

Preparation Time: 10 minutes | Cooking Time: 30 minutes

# Italian Oven Roasted Vegetables

- 8 oz baby bella mushrooms, cleaned, ends trimmed
- 12 oz baby potatoes, scrubbed
- 12 oz Campari tomatoes (grape or cherry tomatoes will work also)
- 2 zucchini (or summer squash), cut into 1-inch pieces
- 10-12 large garlic cloves, peeled
- Olive oil
- 1/2 Tbs dried oregano
- 1 tsp dried thyme
- Salt and pepper
- Freshly grated Parmesan cheese for serving, optional
- Crushed red pepper flakes, optional

- Preheat the oven to 425 degrees F. Lightly grease a large baking sheet.
- Combine the vegetables and garlic in a bowl and mix with a generous amount of olive oil, and the oregano, thyme, salt and pepper. Mix well.
- Spread onto the prepared sheet and bake for 20-25 minutes, or until tender.
- Serve hot garnished with cheese and red pepper flakes, if desired.

Servings: 6 | Serving Size: 8.2 oz

Calories 130 | Fat 6g | Carbohydrates 18g | Protein 4g

Preparation Time: 10 minutes | Cooking Time: 20 minutes

# Mexican-Style Quinoa Salad

- 1/2 cup dry quinoa, pre-rinsed
- 1 cup chicken broth or vegetable broth
- 1 (15-ounce) can black beans, drained and rinsed
- 1 cups salsa
- 1 cup corn kernels
- 1 tsp chili powder
- 1 avocado, peeled and small diced

- Combine the quinoa with broth in a small pot and bring the quinoa to a boil over medium high heat.
- Reduce heat to a simmer and cook, covered, for 12-15 minutes, or until the moisture is absorbed.
- Turn off heat and let the quinoa sit for 5 minutes.
- Add the remaining ingredients, except the avocado, and mix well.
- Season with salt and pepper to taste and top with the avocado immediately before serving.

Servings: 3 | Serving Size: 14.9 oz

Calories 436 | Fat 12g | Carbohydrates 67g | Protein 20g

Preparation Time: 5 minutes | Cooking Time: 15 minutes

# Risotto with Broccoli Rabe, Ricotta & Toasted Zucchini

- 1-1/2 Tbs extra virgin olive oil
- 1 clove garlic, halved
- 1 chili, seeds removed & finely chopped (optional)
- 1 lb broccoli rabe, chopped
- 2 cups rice (the Italian rice varieties to use are Carnaroli, Arborio, Vialone Nano or Roma)
- 1 cup white chicken or vegetable stock
- 4 cups low sodium vegetable broth
- 2 zucchini diced
- 2 oz low fat ricotta cheese, more if needed (can be replaced with Parmesan cheese)
- 1/2 tsp salt
- Pepper

- Sauté the garlic and chili in the olive oil in a large saucepan over medium heat.
- Add the broccoli and cook for 10 minutes, stirring frequently.
- Add the rice and cook for 3 minutes, stirring frequently, to coat the rice with oil.
- Add the chicken or vegetable stock and cook for 2 minutes.
- Add about a third of the broth and stir.
- Cook until almost absorbed and then add another third of the broth.
- Continue to stir to prevent sticking and when the broth is almost absorbed, add the remaining broth.
- Meanwhile, sauté the zucchini in a little more oil for 3-4 minutes, or until golden brown.
- Turn off the heat to the risotto and stir in the ricotta.
- Season to taste with salt and pepper.
- Serve topped with the zucchini.

Servings: 6 | Serving Size: 3/4 cup risotto

Calories 474 | Fat 0g | Carbohydrates 76g | Protein 15g

Preparation Time: 10 minutes | Cooking Time: 25 minutes

# Spinach & Bean Burrito Wrap

- 6 cups baby spinach, loosely packed
- 1 (15 ounce) can black beans, rinsed and drained
- 1 1/2 cups cooked brown rice or Mexican Rice
- 1/2 cup grated cheddar cheese, reduced-fat
- 1/2 cup salsa (recipe), optional Pico de Gallo
- 6 Tbs Greek yogurt, fat-free
- Kosher or sea salt to taste
- 6 large lettuce leaves

- Pulse the spinach in a food processor until finely chopped.
- Heat the black beans and spinach in a large skillet over medium high heat for 3 minutes, or until the spinach is wilted.
- Allow the spinach and bean mixture to cool slightly, so as not to wilt the lettuce.
- Spread a layer of yogurt in the middle of the lettuce.
- Top with the spinach and bean mixture, rice, cheese and salsa.
- Wrap the lettuce leaves and serve immediately.

Servings: 6 | Serving Size: 7 oz

Calories 183 | Fat 4g | Carbohydrates 28g | Protein 10g

Preparation Time: 10 minutes | Cooking Time: 3 minutes

# Spiralized Raw Zucchini Salad with Avocado and Edamame

- 1 medium zucchini, ends trimmed off
- 1/2 lemon
- 1/2 Tbs olive oil
- kosher salt, to taste
- fresh black pepper, to taste
- 2 oz diced avocado (1/2 medium haas)
- 1/3 cup shelled cooked edamame
- 1 basil leaf, minced
- 1 tsp minced chive

- Spiral slice the zucchini and toss with the olive oil, lemon juice, salt and pepper. Mix well.
- Top with the edamame, basil and chives.
- Garnish with avocado and serve immediately.

Servings: 1 | Serving Size: 6 oz (entire recipe)

Calories 144 | Fat 10g | Carbohydrates 16g | Protein 7g

Preparation Time: 10 minutes

# Sweet Potato Quinoa Cakes

- 2 cups cooked quinoa
- 1 medium sweet potato baked
- 2 Tbs applesauce
- 1 egg white
- 1/2 Tbs cinnamon

- Preheat the oven to 400 degrees F. Lightly grease a baking sheet.
- Combine 1 cup of quinoa and the inside of the sweet potato. Mix together well.
- Mix in the egg white, applesauce and cinnamon and mix well.
- Fold in the remaining quinoa and then form into 6 patties.
- Place on the prepared sheet and bake for 10 minutes.
- Flip the patties over and bake for another 10 minutes.
- Serve hot.

Servings: 3 | Serving Size: 2 quinoa cakes

Calories 204 | Fat 0g | Carbohydrates 38g | Protein 8g

Preparation Time: 10 minutes | Cooking Time: 20 minutes

*Note: If desired, use 1 tsp of sage for a more savory cake instead of the cinnamon.

# Summer Vegetable Tian

- 1 medium yellow onion, diced
- 2 cloves garlic, minced
- 1 Tbs olive oil
- 1 medium zucchini, sliced
- 1 medium yellow squash, sliced
- 1 medium potato, sliced
- 1 medium tomato, sliced
- 1 tsp dried thyme
- Salt & pepper
- 1 cup shredded Italian blend cheese
- 1 Tbs chopped parsley, optional garnish

- Preheat the oven to 400 degrees F. Lightly grease an 8x8 inch baking dish.
- Sauté the onion and garlic in a skillet over medium high heat with olive oil for 5 minutes.
- Spread the onion and garlic in the bottom of the pan.
- Stack the zucchini, squash, tomato and potato into the pack vertically in an alternating pattern.
- Season with salt, pepper and thyme.
- Cover and bake for 30 minutes.
- Add the cheese and bake, uncovered, for another 15-20 minutes, or until golden brown.
- Serve, garnished with fresh parsley.

Servings: 4 | Serving Size: 11.3 oz

Calories 182 | Fat 8g | Carbohydrates 18g | Protein 10g

Preparation Time: 15 minutes | Cooking Time: 45 minutes

# Zucchini Noodles with Pesto

- 4 small zucchini, ends trimmed
- 2 cups packed fresh basil leaves
- 2 cloves garlic
- 1/3 cup extra-virgin olive oil
- 2 tsp fresh lemon juice
- 1/4 cup freshly grated Parmesan cheese
- Kosher salt and freshly ground black pepper, to taste
- Cherry or grape tomatoes, optional

- Spiral slice the zucchini noodles and set aside.
- Pulse the basil and garlic in a food processor until coarsely chopped.
- Add the olive oil, while the processor is running, in a slow stream. Scrape the sides down.
- Add the lemon juice and cheese and pulse until well combined.
- Season to taste with salt and pepper.
- Toss the noodles in the pesto and add tomatoes, if using, then serve.

Servings: 4 | Serving Size: 10.3 oz

Calories 311 | Fat 22g | Carbohydrates 26g | Protein 13g

Preparation Time: 15 minutes

*Note: If desired, sauté the zucchini noodles in 1 Tbs of olive oil for 3-4 minutes, or until tender, before mixing with the pesto.

# Zucchini Noodles with Pistachio Pesto

- 1/2 cup pistachios
- 1 cup fresh basil leaves
- 2 cloves garlic, minced
- 1 Tbs lemon juice
- 1/4 cup extra-virgin olive oil
- 1/2 tsp sea salt
- 1/4 cup grated low-fat Parmigiano Reggiano cheese
- 4 large zucchini, spiral sliced

- Combine the pistachios, basil and lemon juice in a food processor and pulse until the nuts are finely chopped.
- With the processor running, drizzle in the olive oil and process until well combined.
- Add in the cheese and process again.
- Toss the zucchini noodles with the pesto and serve.

Servings: 4 | Serving Size: 9.1 oz

Calories 275 | Fat 23g | Carbohydrates 13g | Protein 8g

Preparation Time: 10 minutes

*Note: If desired, sauté the zucchini noodles in 1 Tbs of olive oil for 3-4 minutes, or until tender, before mixing with the pesto.

# Zucchini Noodles with Spinach and Tomatoes

- 3 medium zucchini, spiral sliced
- 3 cups loosely packed spinach leaves, bottom stems removed, divided
- 1-1/2 cups cherry or grape tomatoes, halved
- 1 bunch asparagus, cleaned, hard bottoms (about 2 inches) removed, and cut into 2-inch pieces
- 1 clove garlic, minced
- Spinach-walnut Pesto
- 1/3 cup raw or toasted walnuts
- 1/3 cup freshly grated parmesan
- 1/2 Tbs freshly squeezed lemon juice
- 1/8 tsp salt
- 1/8 tsp black pepper
- 1/4 cup water
- 1/2 Tbs extra-virgin olive oil

- Preheat the oven to 400 degrees F.
- Combine the asparagus, tomatoes, olive oil, salt and pepper in an oven safe skillet and mix well.
- Roast for 15 minutes, or until tender.
- Set aside.
- While the vegetables are cooking, combine 1 ½ cups spinach and the pesto ingredients, except the walnuts, and puree.
- Add the walnuts and blend again until desired texture is reached.
- Combine the pesto and zucchini noodles and add to the veggies. Mix well.
- Heat over low heat for 3-4 minutes, or until warm though. If desired, add ¼ cup water to thin the pesto sauce. Season to taste with salt and pepper.
- Serve hot.

Servings: 6 | Serving Size: 1 1/2 cups

Calories 267 | Fat 0g | Carbohydrates 41g | Protein 8g

Preparation Time: 15 minutes | Cooking Time: 15 minutes

# Greek Roasted Lemon Potatoes

- 1lb red potatoes, unpeeled and cut into chunks
- 4 garlic cloves, minced
- 1/2 Tbs dried oregano
- 2 Tbs olive oil
- 1/3 cup chicken broth or water (if you want to keep it Vegan)
- Juice from 1 large lemon
- Salt and pepper to taste

- Combine all ingredients and mix well.
- Season to taste with additional salt and pepper before serving.

Servings: 4 | Yield: 5.6 oz | Calories 162 | Fat 7g | Carbohydrates 23g | Protein 2g
Preparation Time: 10 minutes | Cooking Time: 45 minutes

# Leek and Cauliflower Gratin

- 3 large leeks, trimmed and sliced
- 1 small head of cauliflower, trimmed and chopped into bite sized pieces
- 2 Tbs butter
- 2 cups reduced fat milk
- 1 cup reduced fat sharp cheddar cheese
- Salt and pepper to taste

- Preheat the oven to 375 degrees F and lightly grease a baking dish.
- Place the vegetables in the prepared pan.
- Heat the butter and 1 ½ cups of milk over medium high heat in a saucepan.
- Season to taste with salt and pepper.
- Whisk in cheese and continue to stir until melted. Season to taste.
- Pour the cheese sauce over the vegetables in the prepared pan.
- Bake, covered, for 25 minutes, or until tender.
- Bake for another 8-10 minutes uncovered and then cool slightly before serving.

Servings: 6 | Yield: 9.1 oz | Calories 166 | Fat 6g | Carbohydrates 19g | Protein 2g
Preparation Time: 5 minutes | Cooking Time: 45 minutes

# Oven Roasted Vegetables

- 3 medium potatoes
- 2 large carrots
- 1 medium onion
- 3 stalks celery
- 3 cloves garlic
- 1/2 tsp salt
- 1/4 tsp pepper
- 1 Tbs lemon juice
- 1 tsp olive oil
- 1 tsp oregano

- Preheat the oven to 350 degrees F.
- Combine all ingredients and mix well.
- Spread onto a baking sheet and bake for 30-45 minutes, stirring at least once, or until the vegetables are tender.

Servings: 4 | Yield: 8.9 oz | Calories 189 | Fat 1g | Carbohydrates 36g | Protein 6g
Preparation Time: 10 minutes | Cooking Time: 30 minutes

# Quinoa Avocado Salad

- 1 cup dry quinoa
- 2 medium avocados
- 3 oz baby spinach
- 8 oz cherry tomatoes
- 3 green onions
- **Dressing**
- 2 cloves garlic, minced
- 2 Tbs red wine vinegar
- 2 Tbs olive oil
- 1/8 tsp salt

- Cook the quinoa according to package directions.
- Combine all ingredients, except avocado, in a large bowl and mix well.
- Add avocado and serve immediately.

Servings: 4 | Yield: 8.3 oz | Calories 384 | Fat 23g | Carbohydrates 39g | Protein 10g
Preparation Time: 10 minutes | Cooking Time: 20 minutes

# Quinoa Baked in Red Peppers

- 8 oz quinoa
- 2 tsp vegetable oil
- 2 cloves garlic, minced
- 1 medium onion, finely diced
- 1 celery stalk, finely diced
- 1 tsp fresh thyme, or 1/2 tsp. dried thyme
- 1 Tbs chopped fresh parsley
- 1/2 cup grated Parmesan cheese
- 2 cups low-sodium chicken broth, divided
- 4 oz provolone cheese, grated and divided
- 6 medium red bell peppers
- 3 tsp dry bread crumbs

- Cook the quinoa according to package directions.
- Meanwhile, preheat the oven to 350 degrees F.
- Sauté the garlic, onion and celery in the oil over medium high heat. Cook for 5-7 minutes, or until tender.
- Add quinoa, thyme, parsley, cheese, salt, ½ cup broth and half of the provolone.
- Slice the tops off the peppers and stuff with the quinoa mixture.
- Place the peppers in a baking dish and pour in the remaining broth.
- Bake for 45 minutes, or until the peppers are tender.

Servings: 6 | Yield: 11.4 oz | Calories 328 | Fat 12g | Carbohydrates 39g | Protein 6g
Preparation Time: 10 minutes | Cooking Time: 1 hour

# Quinoa Tabbouleh

- 1 lemon, juice and zest of
- ½ cup garlic-infused olive oil
- Salt and pepper, to taste
- 3 cups cooked quinoa
- 3 roma tomatoes, seeded and diced
- 1 English cucumber, diced
- 1 bunch Italian parsley, chopped (about ⅔ cups)
- 1 pkg. mint, stems removed and leaves chopped (about ½ cup)
- ¼ cup chives, chopped

- Combine all ingredients and mix well.
- Serve or refrigerate until serving.

Servings: 6 | Yield: 8.9 oz | Calories 296 | Fat 20g | Carbohydrates 26g | Protein 4g

Preparation Time: 25 minutes

# Roasted Green Beans with Lemon, Pine Nuts & Parmigiano

- 1-1/4 lb fresh green beans, rinsed well, stem ends trimmed
- 1 small head garlic
- 1/4 cup plus 2 Tbs. extra-virgin olive oil
- 1-1/2 Tbs finely grated lemon zest (from 1 to 2 medium lemons), plus 2 Tbs. fresh lemon juice
- Kosher salt and freshly cracked black pepper
- 1/3 cup (about 1-1/2 oz.) pine nuts
- 1/4 cup coarsely grated Parmigiano-Reggiano
- 1 Tbs coarsely chopped fresh flat-leaf parsley

- Preheat the oven to 450 degrees F.
- Combine the green beans, garlic, ¼ cup oil, 1 Tbs zest, 1 tsp salt and ½ tsp pepper. Mix well.
- Spread onto a baking sheet and bake for 10 minutes.
- Stir and bake for another 10 minutes.
- Add the remaining oil to the beans and season with salt and pepper. Sprinkle on the remaining seasonings and top with the pine nuts before serving.

Servings: 6 | Yield: 4.3 oz | Calories 81 | Fat 5g | Carbohydrates 8g | Protein 3g
Preparation Time: 10 minutes | Cooking Time: 20 minutes

# Soy and Garlic Sautéed Bok Choy

- 3 heads of bok chok, washed and trimmed
- 4 garlic cloves, minced
- 2 tsp sesame oil
- 3 Tbs reduced sodium soy sauce
- Juice from 1/2 a lime

- Sauté the garlic in the oil for 1 minutes.
- Add the remaining ingredients and cook for an additional 3-4 minutes.

Servings: 4 | Yield: 23.1 oz | Calories 116 | Fat 4g | Carbohydrates 16g | Protein 6g
Preparation Time: 2 minutes | Cooking Time: 5 minutes

# Zucchini Noodles with Creamy Lemon Chive Sauce

- 1 lb zucchini, washed and trimmed
- 1 Tbs fresh lemon juice
- 1 Tbs olive oil
- 1 small garlic clove, minced
- 1/4 cup plain, nonfat Greek yogurt
- 1/4 cup reduced fat sour cream
- 2 Tbs chives, finely chopped
- Salt and pepper to taste

- Combine all ingredients and mix well.
- Season to taste and serve.

Servings: 4 | Yield: 5.3 oz | Calories 79 | Fat 6g | Carbohydrates 5g | Protein 1g

Preparation Time: 10 minutes

# Soup

# Creamy and Spicy Corn Soup

- 5 ears fresh sweet corn
- 1 medium onion, chopped
- 1 tsp olive oil
- 1/2 tsp salt, plus more to taste
- 1/2 a medium yukon gold potato, chopped
- 2-3 cups vegetable stock (the more stock you add, the thinner your soup will be)
- 3 cloves garlic, minced
- 1 tsp cumin
- 1.5 tsp chili powder
- A pinch of cayenne pepper
- 1/4 tsp black pepper

- Cut the corn off the cob.
- Sauté the onion and garlic for 5 minutes in oil in a large pot over medium heat.
- Add the potato and broth and then bring to a boil. Cook for 10 minutes, or until the potatoes are tender.
- Add the corn and cook for an additional 2-3 minutes.
- Add the spices and then puree the soup with a blender.
- Serve with toppings of choice (cilantro, tomatoes, fresh corn, avocado or cheese).

Servings: 4 | Serving Size: 1 1/2 cups

Calories 127 | Fat 0g | Carbohydrates 27g | Protein 4g

Preparation Time: 10 minutes | Cooking Time: 20 minutes

# Hearty Lentil and Vegetable Soup

- 4 cups (1 quart) low-sodium chicken or vegetable broth
- 1 1/2 cups brown lentils
- 2 carrots, peeled and chopped
- 2 stalks celery, sliced
- 1/2 cup chopped onion
- 1 bay leaf
- 2 garlic cloves, minced
- 1/2 tsp cumin
- 1/2 tsp kosher or sea salt
- 1/4 tsp black pepper
- 1 1/2 Tbs olive oil

- Sauté the carrots, onions and celery in the olive oil in a medium stock pot over medium high heat.
- Cook for 5 minutes, or until just beginning to soften.
- Add the garlic and cook for another 30 seconds.
- Stir in the remaining ingredients and then simmer for 25-30 minutes, or until the lentils and vegetables are cooked.

Servings: 6 | Serving Size: 1 1/2 cups

Calories 240 | Fat 0g | Carbohydrates 36g | Protein 15g

Preparation Time: 10 minutes | Cooking Time: 35 minutes

# Sausage and Red Pepper Soup

- 1 lb regular pork sausage
- 1 medium yellow onion, diced
- 3 large red bell peppers, diced
- 4 large garlic cloves, minced
- 10 cup low sodium chicken broth
- 2 cups wild rice, uncooked
- 1-1/2 tsp kosher salt
- 1 tsp dried basil
- 1 tsp dried thyme
- 1 tsp dried savory
- 1 tsp freshly ground black pepper
- 2 oz fresh spinach, chopped

- Brown the sausage in a skillet over medium heat. Be sure to break up the meat while it cooks so no large pieces remain.
- Add the onion and red pepper and cook for another 3-4 minutes.
- Add the garlic and sauté for another minute.
- Combine all ingredients, except the spinach, in a slow cooker and mix well.
- Cook on low for 6-8 hours or high for 3-4 hours.
- Stir in the spinach and season to taste.
- Cook for another 10 minutes, or until the spinach is wilted.
- Serve hot.

Servings: 8 | Serving Size: 16.7 oz

Calories 424 | Fat 21g | Carbohydrates 39g | Protein 21g

Preparation Time: 15 minutes | Cooking Time: 8 hours

# Slow Cooker Chickpea Stew with Apricots

- 2 (15oz) cans chickpeas/garbanzo beans, drained and rinsed
- 1 (28oz) or 2 (14.5oz) cans diced tomatoes
- 1 (15oz) can vegetable broth
- 2 Tbs butter
- 1 onion, finely chopped
- 3 cloves garlic, minced
- ¾ cup turnip, peeled and chopped
- ½ cup dried apricots, chopped
- zest of 1 lemon
- 1 tsp cumin
- ¼ tsp ground coriander
- ½ tsp salt
- pinch of cayenne pepper (or more to taste)
- For Serving:
- cilantro, chopped
- lemon wedges

- Combine all ingredients in a slow cooker and mix well.
- Cook on high for 4 hours or low for 6 hours.
- Season to taste and serve hot with fresh cilantro and lemon wedges.

Servings: 10 | Serving Size: 8.6 oz

Calories 364 | Fat 0g | Carbohydrates 58g | Protein 19g

Preparation Time: 10 minutes | Cooking Time: 6 hours

# Slow Cooker Minestrone

- 1 small onion, diced
- 1 stalk celery, diced
- 2 carrots, peeled and sliced
- 1 zucchini, sliced
- 1 large potato, peeled and cubed
- 2 cups fresh or frozen green beans
- 1 cup fresh or frozen peas
- 2 cups kale, coarsely chopped
- 2 cups vegetable broth or water
- 1 (15 ounce) can diced tomatoes, with liquid
- 1 (15 ounce) can kidney beans, drained and rinsed
- 1/2 cup vegetable or tomato juice
- 1 tsp kosher or sea salt
- 1/4 tsp ground black pepper
- 4 fresh basil leaves, diced
- 1/2 cup Parmigiano Reggiano or Parmesan

- Combine all ingredients, except kale, basil and parmesan in a slow cooker.
- Cook on low for 5-6 hours or high for 3-4 hours.
- Stir in the kale and continue to cook until wilted, about 10 minutes.
- Serve garnished with the basil and cheese.

Servings: 6 | Serving Size: 1 1/4 cups

Calories 240 | Fat 0g | Carbohydrates 22g | Protein 8g

Preparation Time: 15 minutes | Cooking Time: 6 hours

# Slow Cooker Thai Chicken Soup

- 2 Tbs red curry paste
- 2 - 12 ounce cans of coconut milk
- 2 cups chicken stock
- 2 Tbs fish sauce
- 2 Tbs peanut butter
- 1 ½ lbs chicken breasts, cut into 1 ½ inch pieces
- 1 red bell pepper, seeded and sliced into ¼ inch slices
- 1 onion, thinly sliced
- 1 heaping tablespoon fresh ginger, minced
- 1 cup frozen peas, thawed
- 1 Tbs lime juice
- cilantro for garnish

- Combine the curry paste, stock, fish sauce and peanut butter in a slow cooker.
- Place the chicken breast, red pepper, onion and ginger in the cooker and cook on high for 4 hours.
- Stir in the peas and coconut milk and cook for another 30 minutes.
- Stir in the lime juice and serve garnished with cilantro.

Servings: 6 | Serving Size: 14.4 oz

Calories 374 | Fat 17g | Carbohydrates 14g | Protein 41g

Preparation Time: 5 minutes | Cooking Time: 4 hours and 30 minutes

*Note: Be sure to use a natural peanut butter without any sugar added. If necessary, process 1 cup of roasted peanuts in a food processor for 2-3 minutes until peanut butter forms. If needed, add a teaspoon or two of oil until desired consistency is reached. (This works with almonds and cashews as well). The nut butter will last for up to one month in the refrigerator.

# Slow Cooker Tomato, Kale and Quinoa Soup

- 1 cup uncooked quinoa, rinsed thoroughly
- 2 (14.5-ounce) cans petite diced tomatoes
- 1 (15-ounce) can Great Northern beans, drained and rinsed
- 1 onion, diced
- 3 cloves garlic, minced
- 1/2 tsp dried oregano
- 1/2 tsp dried basil
- 1/4 tsp dried rosemary
- 1/4 tsp dried thyme
- 2 bay leaves
- 4 cups vegetable broth
- Kosher salt and freshly ground black pepper, to taste
- 1 bunch kale, stems removed and leaves chopped

- Combine all ingredients, except the kale, in a slow cooker and mix well.
- Season with salt and pepper and then cook on low for 7-8 hours, or high for 4-5 hours.
- Stir in the kale and cook for another 20-30 minutes, or until wilted.
- Season to taste with salt and pepper and serve hot.

Servings: 8 | Serving Size: 7.4 oz

Calories 166 | Fat 2g | Carbohydrates 29g | Protein 8g

Preparation Time: 10 minutes | Cooking Time: 8 hours

# White Chicken Chili

- 2.5 lbs chicken breast or boneless skinless thighs
- 3 cans great northern beans, drained
- 2 8 oz cans mild green chilies, diced
- 1 large yellow onion, diced
- 1 Tbs garlic, minced
- 2 tsp cumin
- 1 tsp chili powder
- ¼ tsp white peper
- 1 Tbs coarse salt, or to taste
- 2 cups chicken broth
- 1 cup milk
- 1/3 cup cilantro, chopped

Combine all the ingredients, except the milk and cilantro, into a slow cooker. Mix well.

Cook on high for 5-6 hours, or until the chicken is tender.

Remove the chicken from the pot and shred with a fork.

Return to the chili and stir in the milk.

Cook for another 10-15 minutes, then serve hot, garnished with cilantro.

Servings: 10 | Serving Size: 9.4 oz

Calories 237 | Fat 3g | Carbohydrates 36g | Protein 18g

Preparation Time: 30 minutes | Cooking Time: 6 hours

# Arugula Caprese Salad

- 5 cups arugula
- 1 cup cherry tomatoes, halved
- 8 oz whole milk fresh mini mozzarella balls, in water (about 24 balls)
- 6 Tbs balsamic vinaigrette dressing
- Salt and pepper as desired

- Combine all ingredients in a large bowl and mix well. Season to taste with salt and pepper before serving.

Servings: 6 | Yield: 3.9 oz | Calories 135 | Fat 8g | Carbohydrates 5g | Protein 1g

Preparation Time: 5 minutes

# Asian Cucumber & Carrot Salad

- 1 large English cucumber
- 2 medium carrots, peeled
- 2 Tbs rice vinegar
- 1 Tbs cider vinegar
- 1 tsp water
- 1 tsp sesame oil
- 1 Tbs sesame seeds

- Spiral slice the cucumber and carrots. Or, use a vegetable peeler to slice them into long strips.
- In a small bowl or jar with lid, mix the vinegar, water and oil.
- Combine the cucumber and carrots in a large bowl and mix with the dressing.
- Serve, garnished with sesame seeds.

Servings: 4 | Yield: 4.7 oz | Calories 53 | Fat 2g | Carbohydrates 10g | Protein 2g

Preparation Time: 10 minutes

# Beet & Spinach Salad

- 2 cups baby spinach leaves, packed
- 1 cup thinly sliced, roasted beets
- 2 Tbs fat free feta
- 1 Tbs chopped walnuts
- 2 Tbs Vinaigrette

- Combine spinach, beets, walnuts and feta and mix well.
- Drizzle on the dressing and serve immediately.

Servings: 1 | Yield: 9.8 oz (entire recipe) | Calories 171 | Fat 7g | Carbohydrates 23g | Protein 5g

Preparation Time: 10 minutes

# Carrot Ginger Soup

- 2 Tbs oil
- 3/4 cup chopped onion
- 1/3 cup fresh ginger, minced
- 6 cups vegetable broth
- 2 lbs carrots, peeled and chopped
- 1 1/2 cups milk (cow or soy)
- 4 Tbs cornstarch, mixed with 1/2 cup of water.
- 1/2 tsp cinnamon, optional
- Salt & Pepper to taste

- Sauté the onions and ginger over medium heat in butter for 5 minutes.
- Add the broth and carrots, then simmer over medium low heat for 20 minutes.
- Puree using a blender or immersion blender.
- Stir in the milk and cook over low heat for 5 minutes.
- Bring to a boil, and stir in the cornstarch before seasoning with cinnamon, salt and pepper.

Servings: 6 | Yield: 17.4 oz | Calories 318 | Fat 9g | Carbohydrates 52g | Protein 8g
Preparation Time: 10 minutes | Cooking Time: 30 minutes

# Classic Creamy Tomato Soup

- 2 lbs fresh tomatoes, chopped
- 1 medium yellow onion chopped
- 1 Tbs light butter
- 1 1/2 cups fat free chicken broth (or vegetable broth)
- 2 bay leaves
- 1/2 cup grated Parmesan cheese
- 1 cup 2% milk
- Salt and pepper to taste

- Sauté the onions in the butter in a large saucepan. Season with salt and cook for 5 minutes.
- Add the tomatoes and ½ cup broth and cook for 8-10 minutes.
- Add the remaining broth and bay leaves. Reduce heat to low and simmer for 10 minutes.
- Add the cheese and milk and stir until the cheese melts, about 2-3 minutes.
- Remove from heat and remove the bay leaves before blending until smooth.

Servings: 4 | Yield: 14.7 oz | Calories 180 | Fat 10g | Carbohydrates 15g | Protein 5g
Preparation Time: 5 minutes | Cooking Time: 30 minutes

# Creamy Shrimp Salad

- 1 lb cooked shrimp, tail off, chopped (defrosted if you are using frozen shrimp)
- 1 cup cherry tomatoes, halved
- 1/4 cup plain, non-fat Greek yogurt
- 2 Tbs reduced fat mayo
- 1/4 cup fresh basil, finely chopped
- 1 tsp garlic powder
- 1 garlic clove, minced
- 1 Tbs fresh lime juice
- Salt and pepper to taste
- *Optional: Romaine lettuce leaves for serving

- Combine all the ingredients and mix well.
- Serve immediately, in lettuce leaves, if desired.

Servings: 4 | Yield: 8.6 oz | Calories 218 | Fat 5g | Carbohydrates 15g | Protein 2g

Preparation Time: 10 minutes

# Easy Asian Quinoa Salad

- **Slaw Ingredients:**
- 1 bag shredded red cabbage (about 4 cups)
- 2 cups cooked quinoa
- 2 cups shredded carrots
- 2/3 cup thinly-sliced green onions
- 2 Tbsp slivered or sliced almonds, toasted
- 2 Tbs sesame seeds

- **Asian Vinaigrette Ingredients:**
- 1/3 cup olive oil
- 3 Tbs rice wine vinegar
- 1 tsp soy sauce
- 1/8 tsp sesame oil
- pinch of salt and black pepper

- Combine the ingredients for the slaw and mix well. Refrigerate until serving.

Servings: 8 | Yield: 6.1 oz | Calories 381 | Fat 29g | Carbohydrates 26g | Protein 7g

Preparation Time: 10 minutes

# Feta, Peach and Fig Salad

- **For the Dressing**
- 3 Tbs extra-virgin olive oil
- 2 Tbs balsamic vinegar
- 1 Tbs maple syrup
- 1/4 tsp salt
- 1/4 tsp black pepper

- **For the Salad**
- 8 cups mixed greens
- 1 Tbs mint leaves, torn
- 1 Tbs basil leaves, torn
- 8 fresh figs, halved
- 2 peaches, halved, pitted and sliced
- 2 Tbsp almonds, sliced
- 1/4 cup reduced fat feta

- Combine the ingredients for the slaw and mix well. Refrigerate until serving.

Servings: 4 | Yield: 8.5 oz | Calories 233 | Fat 13g | Carbohydrates 27g | Protein 5g

Preparation Time: 10 minutes

# Garbanzo Bean Salad

- 2 15oz can garbanzo beans, drained and rinsed
- 1 small red onion, diced
- 1 pint cherry tomatoes, halved
- 1 Tbs olive oil
- 1/4 cup parsley, finely chopped
- 2 Tbs fresh mint, finely chopped
- 1 garlic clove, minced
- Juice from 2 medium sized lemons
- Salt & pepper to taste

- Combine all ingredients in a bowl and mix well.
- Season to taste with additional salt and pepper before serving.

Servings: 8 | Yield: 6.5 oz | Calories 127 | Fat 4g | Carbohydrates 19g | Protein 5g

Preparation Time: 10 minutes

# Garlic Vegetable Soup

- 2 Tbs olive oil
- 2 carrots, chopped
- 2 stalks celery, chopped
- 1/4 medium head cabbage, shredded
- 6 cups chicken broth
- 2 (14.5 ounce) cans peeled and diced tomatoes
- 3 1/2 cups water
- 1 cup wild rice
- 3 cloves garlic, minced
- 1/2 tsp ground black pepper

- Sauté the carrots, celery and cabbage in oil over medium heat in a large pot. Cook for about 8 minutes, stirring frequently.
- Add broth, tomatoes, water and rice then increase heat to high. Bring to a boil, then reduce heat to low and simmer for 1 hour, covered.
- Season with the garlic, salt and pepper to taste and serve.

Servings: 6 | Yield: 21.3 oz | Calories 215 | Fat 7g | Carbohydrates 30g | Protein 6g
Preparation Time: 5 minutes | Cooking Time: 1 hour and 10 minutes

# Greek Chicken Salad

- 2 cup chicken cooked and cubed
- 1 Plum Tomato, small dice
- ¼ cup cucumber, peeled and diced
- 12 Pitted Kalamata Olives
- 1/2 cup feta, crumbled
- 1/2 cup mayonnaise
- 1 Tbs fresh oregano, chopped or 4 tsp. dried oregano
- 2 tsp lemon juice
- Kosher Salt & Black Pepper, to taste

- Combine all ingredients and mix well.
- Season to taste with additional salt and pepper before serving.

Servings: 6 | Yield: 5.3 oz | Calories 122 | Fat 9g | Carbohydrates 6g | Protein 1g

Preparation Time: 15 minutes

# Kale, Strawberry and Avocado Salad

- 5 cups kale, chopped
- 1/2 cup strawberries, sliced
- 1/2 an avocado, chopped
- 1/4 cup sliced almonds
- 2 Tbs olive oil
- 1 Tbs honey
- Juice from 1 lemon
- Salt & pepper to taste

- Whisk together the dressing ingredients.
- Drizzle the dressing over a large bowl with the salad ingredients and mix well before serving.

Servings: 4 | Yield: 5.6 oz | Calories 214 | Fat 15g | Carbohydrates 18g | Protein 6g

Preparation Time: 10 minutes

# Kidney Bean and Cilantro Salad with Vinaigrette

- 1 15-oz. can kidney beans, drained and rinsed
- ½ English cucumbers, chopped
- 1 Medium-sized heirloom tomato, chopped
- 1 bunch fresh cilantro, stems removed, chopped (about 1 ¼ cup)
- 1 red onion, chopped (about 1 cup)
- 1 large lime or lemon, juice of
- 3 Tbs extra virgin olive oil
- 1/4 tsp dry mustard
- ½ tsp fresh garlic paste, or finely chopped garlic
- 1 tsp sumac
- Salt and pepper, to taste

- Combine the vinaigrette ingredients (lime juice, oil, mustard, garlic, sumac and pepper) and mix well.
- Combine the remaining ingredients in a bowl and mix well.
- Drizzle the dressing over the salad and refrigerate for 1 hour before serving.

Servings: 4 | Yield: 5.4 oz | Calories 189 | Fat 11g | Carbohydrates 19g | Protein 5g

Preparation Time: 15 minutes | Calories 189 | Fat 11g | Carbohydrates 19g | Protein 5g

# Quinoa & Grilled Vegetable Salad with Feta, Olives & Oregano

- Kosher salt
- 8 oz quinoa
- 2 Tbs Vegetable oil for the grill
- 2 small Italian eggplants (about 3/4 lb. total), sliced into 1/2-inch-thick rounds
- 1 medium red bell pepper, quartered, stemmed, and seeded
- 1/3 cup plus 2 Tbs. extra-virgin olive oil
- 2 Tbs red-wine vinegar
- 1 Tbs Dijon mustard
- 1/2 small red onion, cut into small dice (about 2/3 cup)
- 1/2 cup crumbled feta (2-1/2 oz.)
- 1/2 cup pitted, coarsely chopped Kalamata olives
- 3 Tbs chopped fresh oregano

- Cook the quinoa according to package directions. Set aside to cool.
- Combine the eggplant, pepper, 2 Tbs oil, salt and pepper.
- Grill on medium high for 2-3 minutes per side.
- Chop the vegetables and whisk together the remaining oil, vinegar and mustard.
- Combine all ingredients and mix well before serving.

Servings: 6 | Yield: 9.4 oz | Calories 285 | Fat 12g | Carbohydrates 38g | Protein 9g
Preparation Time: 10 minutes | Cooking Time: 20 minutes

# Savory Carrot, Ginger Squash Soup

- 2 tsp olive oil
- 4 carrots, peeled and chopped
- 1 small white onion, peeled and chopped
- 1 minced garlic clove
- 3 Tbs diced peeled fresh ginger
- 1 cup cubed peeled butternut squash
- 1 diced peeled apple
- 4 1/2 cups vegetable broth
- 1 1/2 tsp sea salt, plus more to taste
- 12 ounces light coconut milk
- 1 diced peeled pear, for garnish
- 2 tsp minced chives, for garnish

- Sauté the carrots and onions in the oil for 2 minutes.
- Add the garlic, ginger, squash and apple and cook for an additional 3 minutes.
- Add the broth and salt.
- Simmer, covered, for 45 minutes, or until the vegetables are tender.
- Puree, then add the coconut milk and season to taste.
- Garnish with pear and chives before serving.

Servings: 4 | Yield: 22.4 oz | Calories 380 | Fat 13g | Carbohydrates 61g | Protein 10g
Preparation Time: 15 minutes | Cooking Time: 20 minutes

# Southwestern Cobb Salad

- 1 ½ cups mayonnaise
- Juice of 1 large Lime
- 1 Tbs Apple Cider Vinegar
- 1/4 tsp dry mustard
- 1 garlic clove, minced
- ½ tsp Smoked Paprika
- ½ tsp Chili Powder
- 1 tsp Coarse Salt
- 1 Tbs Chives, chopped
- 1 Tbs Cilantro, finely chopped
- 4 large Chicken Breasts
- 2 Tbs Olive Oil
- 1 Tbs Balsamic Vinegar
- Juice of ½ a Lime
- large pinch of Chili Flakes
- ½ tsp Cumin
- ½ tsp Smoked Paprika
- 1 tsp Coarse Salt
- ½ tsp Coarse Ground Pepper
- 6 Small Romaine Hearts, chopped into bite-sized pieces
- ½ cup Cilantro, roughly chopped
- 1 small Red Onion, chopped
- 3 bell peppers, chopped
- 2 Avocados, pitted and sliced into ½" cubes
- ½ cup Pico de Gallo
- 1 can Black Beans, drained

- Combine the mayonnaise, lime juice, vinegar, mustard, garlic, paprika, chili powder, salt, chives and cilantro and mix well.
- Season the chicken with the oil, vinegar, lime juice, chili flakes, cumin, paprika, salt and pepper.
- Grill, bake or fry the chicken until no longer pink.
- Mix the remaining salad ingredients.
- Top with the chicken and drizzle on the dressing before serving.

Servings: 8 | Yield: 8.4 oz | Calories 362 | Fat 22g | Carbohydrates 25g | Protein 8g
Preparation Time: 10 minutes | Cooking Time: 20 minutes

# Spicy Carrot Salad

- 2 tsp ground flaxseed
- 2 Tbs hot water
- 1/4 cup orange juice
- 2 Tbs apple cider vinegar
- 1/2 tsp spanish paprika (spicy, or 1/4 teas. paprika plus 1/4 tsp. cayenne)
- 1/4 tsp cumin
- 4 cups carrots (grated, about 4 large carrots)
- 4 clementines (small seedless oranges, peeled and sectioned)
- 2 Tbs walnuts (optional)

- Combine the flaxseed and water until thick.
- Add the orange juice, vinegar, paprika and cumin. Set aside.
- Combine the carrots, clementines and walnuts.
- Drizzle on the dressing and mix well before serving.

Servings: 4 | Yield: 8.4 oz | Calories 128 | Fat 3g | Carbohydrates 24g | Protein 6g

Preparation Time: 10 minutes

# Warm Mushroom and Asparagus Salad

- 1 lb asparagus spears, trimmed and chopped
- 1 lb mushrooms, sliced
- 4 garlic cloves, chopped
- 3 large scallions, chopped
- 1 Tbs olive oil
- 1 1/2 Tbs balsamic vinegar
- 1 tsp dried thyme
- Salt and pepper to taste

- Blanche the asparagus in boiling water for 2 minutes. Immediately immerse in ice water to stop the cooking.
- Meanwhile, sauté the mushrooms and garlic for 5 minutes.
- Combine the vegetables, vinegar, thyme, salt and pepper. Season to taste and serve.

Servings: 4 | Yield: 8.9 oz | Calories 83 | Fat 4g | Carbohydrates 9g | Protein 4g
Preparation Time: 5 minutes | Cooking Time: 10 minutes

# White Chili

- 2 cans white beans (Great Northern) (14.5 oz each)
- 1 can (12 oz) sweet corn
- 1 Tbs canola oil
- 1 medium jalapeno pepper, minced
- 2 medium poblano pepper, chopped
- 1 large onion, chopped
- 4 cloves garlic, minced
- Salt & Pepper to taste
- 1 Tbs ground cumin
- 1 1/2 tsp ground coriander
- 1 tsp chili powder
- 4 cups vegetable broth
- 2 limes, juiced
- 1/4 cup cilantro leaves, chopped

- Sauté the peppers, onions and garlic for 5 minutes in the oil in a large pot.
- Season to taste with salt, pepper, cumin, coriander and chili powder. Cook for another minute.
- Add the stock, lime juice, beans and corn. Simmer for 20 minutes. Season to taste.
- Add the cilantro and simmer for another 5 minutes.
- Serve hot, garnished with cheese, cilantro and limes.

Servings: 11 | Yield: 8.7 oz | Calories 216 | Fat 4g | Carbohydrates 38g | Protein 7g
Preparation Time: 10 minutes | Cooking Time: 30 minutes

# Vegetarian

# Black Bean and Quinoa Chili Bowl

- 1 (15-ounce) can black beans, drained and rinsed
- 1 clove garlic, minced
- 1/2 cup chopped onions
- 1 Tbs chili powder
- 1 tsp ground cumin
- 1 cup uncooked quinoa (any variety), well rinsed
- 1-1/2 cups corn kernels, frozen, from the cob, or drained from the can
- 1 red bell pepper, stemmed, seeded, and diced
- 1 (14.5 ounce) can diced fire-roasted tomatoes
- 3 cups vegetable broth
- 1 Tbs extra virgin olive oil
- 1/2 tsp kosher or sea salt
- 1/8 tsp cayenne pepper

- Sauté the onion and bell pepper in olive oil over medium heat in a skillet.
- Add the garlic and cook for another 30 seconds, or until fragrant.
- Add in the stock, tomatoes and juice, quinoa, salt, chili powder, cumin and cayenne pepper.
- Simmer for 20 minutes on high, or until the quinoa begins to soften.
- Stir in the corn and black beans and cook for 5 minutes, or until cooked through.
- Serve hot.

Servings: 6 | Serving Size: 1 1/2 cup

Calories 281 | Fat 0g | Carbohydrates 46g | Protein 14g

Preparation Time: 10 minutes | Cooking Time: 30 minutes

# Burrito in a Jar

- 1 cup salsa
- 1 (15 ounce) can black beans, drained
- 1 cup reduced fat cheddar cheese, shredded
- 1/2 cup Greek Yogurt, non-fat (optional non-fat sour cream)

- Place a ¼ cup salsa in the bottom of 4 pint jars.
- Top with a ¼ cup black beans, ¼ cup cheese and 2 Tbsp. of yogurt.
- Serve chilled.

Servings: 4 | Serving Size: 7.2 oz (including the Greek yogurt)

Calories 196 | Fat 3g | Carbohydrates 26g | Protein 18g

Preparation Time: 10 minutes

# Quinoa Stir-Fry

- 1 Tbs extra-virgin olive oil
- 2 tsp sesame seed oil
- 2 cloves garlic, minced
- 4 stalks Bok Choy, leaves removed, sliced into 1/2-inch pieces
- 6 Broccolini or 1 cup broccoli florets
- 2 Tbs (low-sodium) soy sauce, more to taste (optional, Tamari)
- 4 cups cooked and chilled white quinoa (cook according to package instructions)
- 1/4 cup toasted sesame seed

- Heat the oil in a skillet over medium low heat and sauté the garlic for 1 minute.
- Add the bok choy and broccoli and cook, covered, for 5 minutes.
- Remove the broccoli and set aside.
- Stir in the soy sauce and quinoa and continue to cook until heated through.
- Top the quinoa mixture with the broccoli and garnish with sesame seeds.
- Let sit for 5 minutes before serving.

Servings: 6 | Serving Size: 1 cup

Calories 269 | Fat 0g | Carbohydrates 37g | Protein 10g

Preparation Time: 10 minutes | Cooking Time: 10 minutes

# Instant Pot Enchilada Quinoa

- 1 Tbs canola oil
- 1 1/4 cups chopped yellow onion (1 medium)
- 1 1/4 cups chopped red bell pepper (1 medium)
- 3 cloves garlic, minced
- 1 1/2 cups dry quinoa
- 2 1/4 cups vegetable broth
- 1 (14.5 oz) can tomatoes with green chilies, undrained
- 1 (8 oz) can tomato sauce
- 2 Tbs chili powder
- 1 1/2 tsp ground cumin
- Salt and freshly ground black pepper, to taste
- 1 (14.5 oz) can black beans, drained and rinsed
- 1 (14.5 oz) can pinto beans, drained and rinsed
- 1 1/2 cups frozen corn
- 1 1/2 cups cheddar or monterey jack, or Mexican blend cheese
- For serving
- Diced avocados, diced Roma tomatoes, chopped cilantro, lime wedges, chopped green onions (optional)

- Use the sauté function to heat the oil. Once hot, sauté the onion and bell pepper for 3 minutes, then add the garlic and cook for another 30 seconds.
- Add the quinoa, broth, tomatoes, tomato sauce and spices and mix well.
- Cook on high pressure for 1 minute.
- Naturally release the pressure for 10 minutes, then quick release any remaining pressure.
- Stir in the corn and beans and mix well.
- Sprinkle on the cheese and let sit for about 10-15 minutes, covered, until the cheese has melted.
- Serve hot with toppings of choice.

Servings: 8 | Serving Size: 13.4 oz

Calories 391 | Fat 9g | Carbohydrates 60g | Protein 20g

Preparation Time: 10 minutes | Cooking Time: 4 minutes | Inactive Time: 35 minutes

# Mexican Black Bean Casserole

- 2 (15-ounce) cans black beans, drained
- 1/3 cup vegetable broth, low-sodium
- 1 tsp chili powder
- 1 tsp cumin
- 1/2 tsp black pepper
- 1/4 tsp kosher or sea
- 12 oz salsa
- 1 cup shredded Mexican style cheese
- 1/2 cup sliced Jalapeños
- 3 cups cooked rice, for serving, if desired

- Preheat the oven to 375 degrees F.
- Combine the beans, broth, chili powder, cumin, pepper and salt in a bowl and mix well.
- Layer the a quarter of the bean mixture, salsa and cheese in a small casserole dish. Continue to layer until all ingredients have been used.
- Bake for 20 minutes, covered.
- Remove cover and bake for another 10 minutes.
- Garnish with cilantro and serve with rice and other toppings of choice.

Servings: 6 | Serving Size: 11 oz (including rice for serving)

Calories 337 | Fat 6g | Carbohydrates 56g | Protein 18g

Preparation Time: 10 minutes | Cooking Time: 30 minutes

# Quinoa Skillet Supper

- 1 cup (uncooked) quinoa, pre-rinsed
- 2 cups vegetable broth, low sodium
- 2 tsp olive oil
- 2 cloves garlic, minced
- 2/3 cup diced sun-dried tomatoes, packed in olive oil
- 1 tsp dried oregano
- 1/2 tsp black pepper
- 1/2 tsp crushed red pepper flakes
- Kosher or sea salt to taste
- 1 (14 ounce) can small artichoke hearts, drained and quartered

- Combine the quinoa and broth in a saucepan and bring to a boil. Reduce heat to medium and simmer for 15 minutes, or until the liquid is absorbed.
- Meanwhile, sauté the garlic and sundried tomatoes in oil over medium heat in a skillet.
- Add the oregano, black pepper, red pepper flakes, salt and artichokes and cook for another minute.
- Turn off heat and then mix in the quinoa.
- Allow the mixture to rest for 5 minutes before serving.

Servings: 4 | Serving Size: 10.1 oz

Calories 350 | Fat 10g | Carbohydrates 57g | Protein 14g

Preparation Time: 10 minutes | Cooking Time: 15 minutes

# Roasted Asparagus with Tomato, Halloumi Cheese and Sherry Vinaigrette

- 1.5 lb asparagus, hard end trimmed
- alt
- Extra Virgin Olive Oil
- 8 oz Halloumi cheese, sliced into squares 1/2 inch in thickness
- 3 cups grape tomatoes, halved
- 15 large basil leaves, torn

- For the Sherry Vinaigrette
- 1/4 cup sherry reserve vinegar
- 1/4 cup extra virgin olive oil
- 1/2 tsp garlic powder
- salt and pepper

- Preheat the oven to 400 degrees F.
- Spread the asparagus onto a large baking sheet and drizzle with olive oil.
- Season with salt and then roast for 15-20 minutes.
- Meanwhile, heat 2 Tbs of oil over medium heat in a large skillet.
- Fry the halloumi cheese for 1-2 minutes, turning once.
- Once golden brown, remove and set aside.
- Whisk together the vinaigrette ingredients and then set aside.
- Combine the tomatoes and hallouimi and then drizzle on the vinaigrette.
- Serve the asparagus topped with the tomato mixture and garnished with basil.

Servings: 4 | Serving Size: 14.4 oz

Calories 430 | Fat 34g | Carbohydrates 23g | Protein 17g

Preparation Time: 10 minutes | Cooking Time: 25 minutes

*Note: Greek Feta can be used in place of Hallouimi but should not be fried. Instead, just toss together the tomatoes, feta and dressing.

# Roasted Vegetable Quinoa Bowls

- For the vegetables:
- 1 large sweet potato, chopped into 1/2-inch pieces
- 2 cups broccoli florets
- 2 cups cauliflower florets
- 2 cups Brussels sprouts, cut in half
- 1/2 red onion, sliced
- 1-2 tablespoons olive oil
- Salt and black pepper, to taste
- 3 cups chopped kale

- For the Quinoa:
- 1 cup quinoa, rinsed
- 2 cups vegetable broth
- pinch of salt
- For the Lemon Tahini Dressing:
- 1/3 cup tahini
- 1 clove garlic
- 4 Tbs lemon juice
- 1/3 cup warm water
- Salt and pepper, to taste

- Preheat the oven to 400 degrees F.
- Spread the vegetables in a single layer on two baking sheets.
- Drizzle with olive oil and season with salt and pepper.
- Bake for 20 minutes, or until tender.
- Meanwhile, combine the chicken broth, quinoa and salt in a saucepan.
- Bring to a boil and then reduce heat and cook on low, covered, for 15 minutes.
- Let stand for 5 minutes, and then fluff with a fork.
- Whisk together the dressing ingredients and season to taste with salt and pepper.
- Place the quinoa in bowls, then top with the vegetables and kale.
- Drizzle on the dressing and serve.

Servings: 4 | Serving Size: 16 oz

Calories 424 | Fat 17g | Carbohydrates 55g | Protein 18g

Preparation Time: 20 minutes | Cooking Time: 40 minutes

# Southwestern Broccoli & Potato Casserole

- 4 medium red potatoes
- 2 cups small broccoli florets
- 1/2 tsp black pepper
- 1/2 tsp kosher or sea salt
- ½ cup vegetable broth
- 1 1/2 cups full-fat Greek yogurt, (optional sour cream)
- 1 (4-ounce) can diced green chiles
- 3/4 cups shredded cheddar cheese, reduced-fat
- 3/4 cups shredded mozzarella, part-skim
- 3 green onions, sliced

- Preheat the oven to 400 degrees F.
- Pierce the potatoes with a fork and then wrap the potatoes in foil and bake for 45 minutes, or until tender.
- Cool the potatoes until they can be easily handled and chop the potatoes into cubes.
- Combine the potatoes, broccoli, half of the cheese, pepper and salt in a 9x13-inch casserole pan.
- Combine the broth, yogurt and green chilies.
- Pour the mixture over the potatoes and broccoli and sprinkle on the remaining cheese.
- Bake, covered, for 20 minutes, then uncover and bake for another 10 minutes, or until the cheese is melted and bubbly.
- Garnish with green onions before serving.

Servings: 8 | Serving Size: 6.5 oz

Calories 171 | Fat 7g | Carbohydrates 17g | Protein 11g

Preparation Time: 15 minutes | Cooking Time: 1 hour and 20 minutes

*Note: If desired, potatoes can be cooked in the microwave instead of baked to speed the cooking process.

# Black Bean & Sweet Potato Quinoa

- 1 large sweet potato, peeled and diced
- 1 tsp olive oil
- ½ tsp chili powder
- ¼ tsp cumin
- ¼ tsp salt
- **Quinoa:**
- ¾ cup quinoa
- 1 ¾ cup water
- ½ tsp chili powder
- ½ tsp cumin
- ¼ tsp garlic powder
- ½ lime, juiced
- 2 Tbs cilantro, chopped
- **Cilantro Cream:**
- ½ cup plain Greek yogurt
- ¼ cup cilantro, chopped
- ½ lime, juiced
- pinch salt, garlic powder and chili powder
- **Also Needed:**
- 1 cup black beans, rinsed and drained

- Preheat the oven to 425 degrees F and lightly grease a baking sheet.
- Seaosn the sweet potato with the spices and spread onto the prepared sheet.
- Bake for 12-15 minute,s or until tender.
- Meanwhile, combine the quinoa and water and bring to a boil.
- Reduce heat to a simmer, and cover. Cook for 15 minute.s
- Whisk together the cilantro cream sauce ingredients and set aside.
- Top the quinoa with the black beans and roasted sweet potato, then drizzle on the cilantro cream.
- Serve warm.

Servings: 4 | Yield: 9.7 oz | Calories 222 | Fat 4g | Carbohydrates 40g | Protein 8g
Preparation Time: 20 minutes | Cooking Time: 20 minutes

# Carrot and Spinach Quinoa Pilaf

- 2 tsp olive oil
- 1/2 onion, chopped
- 1 cup quinoa
- 2 cups water
- 2 Tbs vegetarian chicken-flavored bouillon granules
- 1 tsp ground black pepper
- 1 tsp thyme
- 1 carrot, chopped
- 1 tomato, chopped
- 1 cup baby spinach

- Sauté the onion in oil over medium high heat for about 5 minutes, or until tender.
- Reduce heat to medium low and stir in the quinoa. Cook for 2 minutes, then add the water, bouillon, pepper and thyme.
- Bring to a boil and then reduce heat to low and simmer for 5 minutes. Stir in the carrots and cook for another 10 minutes, or until the water is absorbed.
- Remove from the heat and stir in the tomatoes and spinach. Let the mixture rest for about 2 minutes, or until the tomatoes are tender and the spinach is wilted.

Servings: 3 | Yield: 15.2 oz | Calories 294 | Fat 8g | Carbohydrates 48g | Protein 9g
Preparation Time: 10 minutes | Cooking Time: 25 minutes

# Chile Con Queso Recipe

- 1 10-ounce can diced tomatoes, drained
- 1/2 cup diced Anaheim chilies
- 1 3/4 cups reduced fat shredded sharp Cheddar
- 1 1/4 cups skim milk
- 1 large onion, chopped
- 3 cloves garlic, minced
- 1/4 cup fresh cilantro, chopped
- 1/4 cup sliced green onions
- 2 tsp lime juice
- 1 tsp salt
- 1/8 tsp black pepper
- 1 tsp ground cumin
- 1 tsp chili powder

- Sauté the onions and garlic in cooking spray over medium heat for 4-5 minutes.
- Add the milk and bring to a simmer.
- Stir in the cheese until melted.
- Add the remaining ingredients and cook for an additional 2-3 minutes, or until cooked through.
- Serve hot, garnished with additional cilantro, if desired.

Servings: 12 | Yield: 3.6 oz | Calories 53 | Fat 1g | Carbohydrates 5g | Protein 1g
Preparation Time: 5 minutes | Cooking Time: 15 minutes

# Indian Vegetable Curry

- 1 cup unsweetened coconut milk
- 12 oz cauliflower florets, cut into bite-size pieces (about 3 cups)
- 1 large carrot, sliced 1/4 inch thick on the diagonal
- 1 medium yellow onion, halved and thinly sliced lengthwise
- 1 Tbs minced fresh ginger
- 2 tsp minced garlic
- 2 tsp hot curry powder, such as Madras
- Kosher salt
- 3 oz baby spinach (about 3 lightly packed cups)
- 1 15-oz. can chickpeas, drained and rinsed
- 2 medium plum tomatoes, cut into 1/2-inch dice
- 3 Tbs chopped fresh cilantro

- In a 12-inch skillet set over medium-low heat, stir together the coconut milk, cauliflower, carrot, onion, ginger, garlic, curry powder, and 1 tsp. salt. Raise the heat to high and bring to a boil; reduce to a simmer, cover, and cook, stirring often, until the cauliflower is tender when pierced with a knife, about 10 minutes. (If the pan looks dry, stir in water 1/4 cup at a time.)
- Stir in the spinach, chickpeas, and tomatoes and continue to cook until the chickpeas are heated through and the spinach is wilted, about 5 minutes. Stir in the cilantro, season to taste with salt, and serve.

Servings: 6 | Yield: 8.3 oz | Calories 140 | Fat 6g | Carbohydrates 18g | Protein 6g
**Preparation Time: 5 minutes | Cooking Time: 20 minutes**

# Mushroom & Quinoa Sauté

- 1 cup quinoa, rinsed
- 1 lb mushrooms, sliced
- 1 small onion, finely diced
- 1 Tbs light butter
- 4 cloves garlic, minced
- 1 tsp dried thyme
- Salt & pepper to taste

- Prepare the quinoa according to package directions.
- Meanwhile, sauté the onion, garlic, mushroom and thyme for 5 minutes over medium high heat.
- Add the quinoa and season with salt and pepper to taste.

Servings: 4 | Yield: 6.8 oz | Calories 216 | Fat 5g | Carbohydrates 35g | Protein 5g
Preparation Time: 5 minutes | Cooking Time: 20 minutes

# Quinoa with Pomegranates & Butternut Squash

- 1 cup quinoa, cooked
- 1/2 cup butternut squash, cubed and cooked
- 2 Tbs pomegranate seeds
- 1 Tbs orange zest
- 1 Tbs olive oil
- 2 Tbs orange juice
- Salt and pepper to taste

- Combine all ingredients and mix well.
- Refrigerate until serving.

Servings: 2 | Yield: 5.8 oz | Calories 205 | Fat 9g | Carbohydrates 28g | Protein 4g

Preparation Time: 10 minutes

# Special Bonus Reminder

## Are you interested in receiving over 600 delicious recipes for FREE?

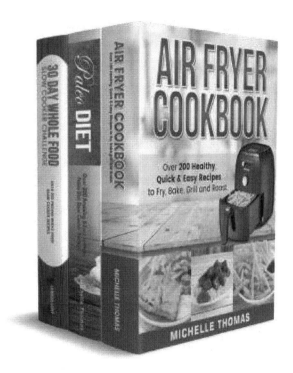

Only sign up for the cookbook box set if you are ready to be absolutely amazed with over 600 proven, delicious and easy to make recipes.

CLICK HERE or copy-paste www.bit.ly/2Ho82AH to get the free box set.

Happy cooking!

Made in the USA
Middletown, DE
11 September 2018